*Thomas Conolly (1823–76) of Castletown House
and the social networking of power*

T0048976

Maynooth Studies in Local History

SERIES EDITOR Michael Potterton

This is one of six volumes in the Maynooth Studies in Local History series for 2022. It is also my first year as series editor, having taken over the role from the irreplaceable Raymond Gillespie, who held that position from 1995 to 2021, overseeing the publication of a veritable treasure trove of studies in those 27 years. Raymond established the series with Irish Academic Press as a direct result of the enormous success of the Maynooth MA in Local History programme, which began in 1992. Under Raymond's supervision, some 153 volumes were produced, authored by 140 different scholars (94 men and 46 women). The first volume, on education in nineteenth-century Meath, was written by Paul Connell, and the 153rd, on the Dublin Cattle Market in the 1950s and 1960s, was by Declan O'Brien. Eleven people have each contributed two volumes to the series, while Terry Dooley is the only person to have written three.

The remarkable collection now covers some 1,500 years of history across 31 counties, dealing variously with aspects of agriculture and fishing, architecture, crime and punishment, death and burial, economy and trade, education, famine, gender, healthcare, industry, language and literature, migration, music and the arts, politics, religion, society, travel and communication, urban development, war and much more besides. I am grateful to Raymond for entrusting the series to me, and to Four Courts Press for not vetoing the appointment. Together, I am sure that we can build on the sound foundations established over more than quarter of a century of diligent work.

The current crop of titles takes us from a broad look at religion and society in medieval Galway to a very specific and tragic event in Knockcroghery village on the night of 20 June 1921. En route we witness the gradual dismantling of Irish lordship in early modern north Co. Cork, and the development of nursing and midwifery in Co. Tipperary at the turn of the twentieth century. Finally, we have biographical sketches of two remarkable men of the nineteenth century – Thomas Conolly (1823–76) of Castletown House in Co. Kildare and botanist Nathaniel Colgan (1851–1919) of Dublin.

While the genesis and home of this series lie firmly at Maynooth, it is a mark of its appeal, its breadth and its inclusivity that this year's contributors are drawn from Carlow College, Glenstal Abbey, NUI Galway, Trinity College Dublin and the University of Limerick as well as Maynooth University.

Maynooth Studies in Local History: Number 159

Thomas Conolly (1823–76) of Castletown House and the social networking of power

Suzanne M. Pegley

FOUR COURTS PRESS

Set in 11.5pt on 13.5pt Bembo by
Carrigboy Typesetting Services for
FOUR COURTS PRESS LTD
7 Malpas Street, Dublin 8, Ireland
www.fourcourtspress.ie
and in North America for
FOUR COURTS PRESS
c/o IPG, 814 N Franklin Street, Chicago, IL 60610

© Suzanne M. Pegley 2022

ISBN 978-1-80151-034-9

All rights reserved. Without limiting the rights under
copyright reserved alone, no part of this publication may
be reproduced, stored in or introduced into a retrieval system,
or transmitted, in any form or by any means (electronic,
mechanical, photocopying, recording or otherwise), without
the prior written permission of both the copyright
owner and the above publisher of this book.

Printed in Ireland
by SprintPrint, Dublin

Contents

Acknowledgments

This study would never have been completed without the direction and encouragement of my supervisor Ronan Foley. I would also like to thank Prof. Mary Gilmartin for her contribution to the final drafts. Thanks as well to Mary Kelly and Shelagh Waddington for their thoughtful comments on the thesis in 2018.

As the research evolved, I visited the main repositories and I would like to thank those who assisted me. Rebecca Hayes, at the Grand Masonic Hall, Molesworth Street in Dublin, and Natasha Serns at the Royal Dublin Society, who both willingly opened their archives to me. I would like to especially thank the staff of the Kildare Street and University Club, but particularly Susie Harrington, the office manager. During the period I spent in their archive I was welcomed and treated with great courtesy and with lunches they most thoughtfully provided. I want to also thank Felix Larkin and Ian d'Alton of the Library Committee, who sponsored my time in the club.

Thomas Conolly's diaries that are so pivotal to the study are part of the collection of the late Desmond Guinness who generously allowed me access. I would also like to thank David Griffin, the now-retired director of the Irish Architectural Archive that holds Conolly's other three diaries.

I cannot fail to mention the National Library of Ireland's manuscripts library and Trinity College Dublin's Manuscript and Rare Books 'hidden' archive. I would like to thank Maynooth University's John Paul II Library and their archivist Nicola Kelly of the Castletown Archive at Castletown House. She was most generous in her willingness to discuss the research and suggest relevant items. I very much appreciate her collegiality. The other library that was extremely helpful was that of Blackhall Place, that provided material otherwise unavailable.

Others who were key and who provided material that added significantly to the core of the study are Christopher Shuldham Shaw and Dean Crowley, two gentlemen, one in England and the other in New Zealand, who have been invaluable in helping me to develop the Shaw Conolly family connection, June Stuart for the Street Directories, and Jeanne Meldon Walsh, co-director of the Castletown Foundation, who allowed me to quote from her unpublished lecture on the history of Castletown House. Thanks to Turtle Bunbury for the photographs of the Rathdonnell Collection and finally solicitor Paul Kerrigan. I would like to sincerely thank these individuals and many more that room does not allow for.

In the same vein are my family and friends who were tolerant and supportive throughout the research and writing of this study. Included are Dr Aiden O'Boyle, Dr Brendan Twomey, Linda Curran, Patricia Donohoe and Dr Ian d'Alton. By far the greatest of these was my husband Charlie, for the roof over our head and the food on the table. *Deo Gratis.*

Thomas Conolly: timeline

1823 born to Catherine Ponsonby Barker and Edward Michael. Parents may have been living at Castletown but TC's baptism not recorded in local church.

1845 diary of 1870 reports TC was touring the Continent in this year

1849 father died; TC put himself up as member for Ballyshannon

1852 elected as member for Ballyshannon

1853 sister Louisa Augusta drowned while sea bathing at Ardgillan, Co. Dublin. LA left two children and husband, the earl of Langford, who died 1854

1860 began to refurbish Castletown (house and parkland). Impressive garden house and green house in kitchen garden. Planted lime walk from house eastwards toward Wonderful Barn

1864 visited Paris; took part in military manoeuvres with French Army

1864/5 set out with others to run Yankee blockade of southern states of America. Remained there until early 1865, returning to UK to continue political career

1868 married Sarah Eliza Shaw in lavish highly publicized event

1870/1 with Sarah Conolly travelled to Italy for three months with baby Thomas. Three further children between 1872 and 1874: Catherine, William, Edward

1875 health began to fail; sold off hunters and dairy herd

1876 died of renal failure, 10 August

Introduction

This biography of Thomas Conolly (1823–76) provides a representative example of the type of individuals who made up the power network in Ireland in the nineteenth century and earlier. The Conolly family offer a classic example of the 'power elite'. This is the first time a history of Castletown has been attempted that considers the house and the family between the death of the first Thomas Conolly, known as Squire Tom, in 1803 and the death of the second Thomas Conolly in 1876. Filling the gap in the written history of Castletown is at the heart of this quest to rediscover what could be described as the 'lost' nineteenth century. The only extant source for the life of this second Thomas are his few remaining private diaries. This source consists of five diaries written between 1853 and 1864 in the collection of the late Desmond Guinness, and three more lodged in the Irish Architectural Archive. These fragments offer a limited glimpse of Conolly as he went about his everyday life.

The Conolly family are an illuminating prism through which to study the effects of power on the wider population and the eventual weakening and decline of the Protestant elite. In the mid-seventeenth century the Donegal-based Conolly family, as with many other Roman Catholic families, had made a decision to convert to Protestantism and subsequently became deeply embedded in the power structure of the time. By using biographical material associated with the Conollys, one can trace the rise and decline in the operation of that power.

Thomas Conolly, although an elite member of an elite Protestant landowning community, played only a minor part in the history of Ireland. Nevertheless, he lived life socially and politically to the fullest as a resident landlord and he was remembered by his contemporaries and his tenants with fondness. He drew upon the capital of his family but his position in the mid-Victorian period has become a footnote in the established story of the Conolly family. This has as much to do with his lack of a fortune as the times he lived in. As the owner of

Castletown House, the first great Palladian mansion in Ireland, he was among the few remaining classic Protestant ascendancy landowners of a great house active in the nineteenth century. In framing the social networks he occupied, Castletown can be identified as an important setting for his story.

From the lofty eighteenth-century heights of William Conolly's position as Speaker of the Irish House of Commons, a proto-prime-ministerial position, with highly influential political power, the family's slow decline is reflected in Thomas Conolly's eventual position as a 'jobbing' MP, who had difficulty in retaining his seat. Using Conolly as a case study for his family throws new light on a critical period in the history of Ireland in the mid-nineteenth century and serves as a useful insight into the relational geographies of the influential power elite. It also supports the blending of the eighteenth- and nineteenth-century family history into the wider mobile and shifting networks within which it operated. On a deeper level, the book considers how power was used as a commodity and traded within and between the hierarchies of the time by examining the social networks of the small cohort of Irish power elite. They provide a model for how these networks operated, facilitating the transfer and maintenance of power, not only in Ireland but in any hierarchal structure either historically or in the corporate world today. In general, historians and historical geographers have failed to fully recognize the integrated nature of the social network and the reproduction of power.

Chapter 1 considers the family history and chapter 2 the core of Thomas Conolly's biography, putting into context the family's place in the social and political power structure. Chapter 3 looks at how the connections of the establishment, through the social and political activities of Thomas Conolly, re-enforced the networks of power and social connection.

1. The Conollys and Castletown House

In 1709, Speaker William Conolly bought the lands near Celbridge, Co. Kildare, on the river Liffey from the earls of Limerick. The estate included a substantial house but not one that conveyed the statement of power of financial and cultural capital that Conolly wished to demonstrate, one which would signify 'a sense of security and confidence in the future'.[1] As a result, he set about creating a significant cultural statement in the shape of a Palladian-style house, which he named Castletown (fig. 1.1) and that some compared to an Italian palace. The Speaker poured his efforts and his fortune into the building and, without children, this would be his splendid legacy. Even in its unfinished state it would be a 'venue for political intrigue and entertainment ... hosting successive lords lieutenant'.[2]

After the Speaker's death in 1729, it became apparent that he had invested heavily in the as-yet unfinished house and, compounding the difficulties, he left other major debts. As a result, his fortune was greatly depleted. His wife Katherine Conyngham lived and entertained in the largely undecorated mansion for the remaining twenty-three years of her life but, to magnify the financial difficulties, Katherine's jointure[3] had been a generous €5,000 per annum. This she spent freely, in her long widowhood, without re-investing in any improvements at Castletown. By the time of her death in 1752, there was little money left.[4] The Speaker's nephew and heir, also William, struggled to meet the debts of his uncle and to manage the estate at arm's length.[5] Dying in 1754 soon after his aunt, the debts fell onto the shoulders of his son and the Speaker's great nephew, Thomas Conolly (1738–1803). Thomas, who came to be known as Squire Tom, also struggled with his great-uncle's debts and with added burdens handed down by his father that involved responsibility of his mother's jointure and the future marriage settlements of his six sisters.[6] The house remained much as it had in Katherine's time until it

1.1 Castletown House, 2017

was refurbished around the period of the marriage in 1758 of Thomas
to Lady Louisa Lennox, the daughter of the duke of Richmond,
whose elder sister Emily was married to the duke of Leinster. This
shows how inter-marriage within the ascendency network often
acted as a cementing of relationships as well as a financial lifeboat.
Squire Tom, with the advice of the duke of Leinster, who was
apparently the instigator of the project, began the reordering and
ornamenting of the house and the demesne.[7] Marrying Louisa for
love did nothing to improve his finances, and their childlessness,
while undoubtedly upsetting personally, did nothing to encourage
reinvestment in the estate. The magnificent redecorating and the
social whirl that accompanied the period of their early married life
did nothing to ease the debts, and these financial burdens, coupled
with his family financial commitments, are the background to the
nineteenth-century decline.

    With Squire Tom, the power of the family, while significant, was
no longer at the prestigious level of his great-uncle, the Speaker. He
was elected as MP for Malmsby, England, between 1759 and 1768,
and for Chichester from 1768 to 1780, with the influence of his

sister-in-law's husband Henry Fox. Simultaneously, he was MP for Ballyshannon and Londonderry between 1761 and 1800. Holding three elected positions at the same time between two countries must have presented conflicting political stances, not to mention the social and geographical differences.

Coupled with Squire Tom's less-than-top-class career were the consequences of economic insecurity, which meant that the borrowings from friends and the mortgaging of lands, particularly in Ulster, moved the family deeper into financial burden. When the fortune, promised by his uncle the earl of Wentworth, went to another family member, this added to his difficulties.[8] Details about the family's financial circumstances can be found in the *History of parliament, 1820–1832*, which indicates that 'the estate was encumbered by debts amounting to nearly £50,000 in 1797'.[9] Nevertheless, this did nothing to stop the Conollys from enjoying their usual lifestyles, although the variety of activities they enjoyed may have been restricted. A lack of fortune might prevent individuals from joining the elite hierarchy but the lack by those already well established over the generations did not stop their continued involvement in the social and leisure activities of their social equals, and the network of social contact between elites remained. Towards the end of his life, one of many complex decisions made by Squire Tom was to appoint an heir, having had no children with Louisa. The connection for inheritance came through one of his five sisters, Harriet, first wife of the Rt Hon. John Staples. In 1785, their daughter Louisa Ann married Thomas Pakenham (1757–1836),[10] the younger son of Thomas first Lord Longford, who would later become an admiral and earn himself a knighthood.[11] A family tree (table 1) shown here may clarify some of the family connections.

Admiral Sir Thomas Pakenham and Louisa Ann had ten children and their eldest son Edward Michael, born in 1789, was named after his uncle, the second Lord Longford. As Squire Tom's sister Harriet's grandson, Edward Michael, one of Tom's four nephews, was chosen as his heir with the hope that he would 'be resident in Ireland as their ancestor Mr Speaker Conolly the original and honest maker of my fortune'.[12] Like other men in similar circumstances who wished to see their family name continue, Squire Tom required that his heir must change his name to Conolly; failing this the inheritance would pass to

Thomas Pakenham (1714–66)   1st Baron Longford
m. Elizabeth Cuffe (1719–94)

- Robert d. 1775
- Edward Michael 1743–92 2nd Baron Longford
- Frances 1744–76
- Helena 1745–77
- Mary 1749–75
- William 1756–69
- **Thomas** 1757–1836 m. Louisa Ann Staples d. 1833

Children of Thomas:
- **Edward Michael** 1786–1849
- Thomas 1787–1846
- John 1790–1876
- Henrietta 1795–1869
- Richard 1797–1868
- Robert 1799–1883
- Sarah d. 1802

Edward Michael m. Catherine Jane Ponsonby Barker d. 1861

Children:
- Chambre Brabazone 1820–35
- Louisa Augusta 1822–53
- **Thomas Conolly** 1823–76 m. Sarah Eliza Shaw 1846–1921
- Henrietta 1825
- Frederick William 1826
- Arthur Wellesley 1828–54
- John Augustus 1829–88
- Mary Margaret 1830–91
- Francis Catherine 1833–74
- Richard 1834–70

Children of Thomas Conolly:
- Infant son 1869
- Thomas 1870–1900
- Catherine 1871–1947
- William 1872–95
- Edward Michael 1874–1956

Table 1. Pakenham/Conolly family tree

the next candidate in the list of five people.[13] When Squire Tom died in 1803, Edward Michael at age 16 became the de facto heir. His father, Admiral Sir Thomas and Squire Tom's other trustee Lord Clancarty assisted Lady Louisa with her financial affairs and the running of the estate during the remainder of her life. Indeed, Squire Tom's niece Louisa Ann Staples Pakenham was such a favourite of Lady Louisa that the Pakenhams were invited to live at Castletown. Among Lady Louisa's papers, in a letter to her sister, is some evidence to confirm this where she discussed the manufacture of a 'pretty watch' embellished by '82 diamonds' for Louisa Ann Staples.[14] Admiral Sir Thomas, the younger son of the earl of Longford of Coolure, built a comfortable house on the shores of Lough Derravaragh close to Castlepollard, Co. Westmeath, in the 1780s adjacent to the lands of his brother the earl at Tullynally.[15]

Following the death of Louisa in 1821, Edward Michael duly changed his name from Pakenham to Pakenham Conolly.[16] The financial burden hinted at earlier had remained unresolved and even increased during the eighteen years of Lady Louisa's widowhood. At age 35, when he took over the running of the estate, Edward Michael had been handed something of a poisoned chalice with the weighty historical financial burdens, and Castletown fell into a steady and largely uneventful existence despite its splendour for the next several decades.

Edward Michael Conolly was a captain in the Royal Artillery, a lieutenant colonel of the Donegal Militia, MP for Ballyshannon (1831–49) and high sheriff of Donegal and Kildare. He married Catherine Jane Ponsonby Barker in 1819 and the couple had ten or eleven children between c.1822 and 1834. There is little evidence of the lifestyle of Edward Michael and Catherine Jane at Castletown at this time. Revd Robert Pakenham, rector of Christ Church, Celbridge, the Church of Ireland church at the end of Castletown avenue, was Conolly's uncle.[17] He and his family must have been regular visitors to Castletown if not residents, since the address given in the parish register of their children's births was Castletown. Besides Robert and his family, other Pakenham names appear in the register of the church, which would indicate the possibility of more members of his family living in the area.

Only a single bank book for the year 1840–1, from La Touche and Co., and household account books for 1828–41 offer any other personal details about Edward Michael.[18] These reveal, indirectly, some comings and goings at Castletown Demesne and a slender indication of his engagement with the Donegal property and the wider community. Despite his historic financial difficulties, he had another fine house at Cliff, Co. Donegal. This was the designated residence for his Donegal constituency, built in 1810 by his father Thomas, despite the family's apparent lack of money.[19]

Edward Michael's obituary was lavish in its praise for him as a resident landlord who was 'deservedly beloved by a numerous tenantry to whom his active benevolence justly endeared him. He was unceasing in his attention to their welfare and spared neither trouble or expense [in the] advancement of their interest or the promotion of that happiness'.[20] While these heartfelt obituaries were well meaning, they were not always written with the greatest accuracy and were prone to exaggeration; by complimenting the deceased wherever possible they conformed to the social niceties of the day.

2. Thomas Conolly, 1823–76

On the death of Edward Michael, his eldest son Thomas (1823–76) (fig. 2.1) succeeded to Castletown and would declare his candidacy for the family constituency in Donegal in the month of his father's death. From the start, the financial difficulties of the past and the seeds of later difficulties were evident and he was 'obliged to sell off large parts of the family estates to discharge his father's debts', nevertheless, this second Thomas Conolly of Castletown lived recklessly and 'exceeded the extravagances of his eighteenth-century namesake in his equipage and entertainments'.[1] The brief biography of his life and events that he engaged in will stand as an example of the social networks of the power elite.

Thomas Conolly, born in 1823, inherited Castletown at age 25. His bachelor ways, involving a busy social life and a full hunting schedule, on top of his responsibilities as MP, meant he spent little time at home. He became a Conservative MP for Co. Donegal from 1849, spending brief times at his residence at Cliff.[2] He also held the positions of deputy lieutenant and justice of the peace for Donegal and Kildare, high sheriff of Co. Donegal in 1848 and was a long-serving member of the Donegal Grand Jury.

Conolly's political career began on the cusp of a changing political landscape when the shift in power away from the landowners was just beginning. Up to the 1870s, the political power of elite landowners was still impressive. In the 1840s when he entered politics these old landed power elites were still the political representatives at Westminster, but in the coming decades power would shift into the hands of the new Roman Catholic political movements and their own representative elites. In 1874, the last election before his death, and the first to employ a secret ballot, Conolly only just managed to secure his Donegal seat.

Conolly's references to his involvement in his role as MP in his diaries are somewhat slim. He was first elected to his father's seat in May 1849 and made his 'maiden' speech in March of that year. The

2.1 Thomas Conolly, 1865
(Kildare Hunt Album)

occasional references in his diary to the House of Commons only
include remarks about being at the house to a late hour and infrequent
brief comments about the debates he participated in. Conolly's visits
to Donegal, as MP for Ballyshannon, while never recorded explicitly
as constituency business, would probably have been occurring
throughout the year irrespective of the season.

Between the conclusion of the Famine (when he was first elected)
and 1876 (when he died), Ireland changed substantially. It had been a
torrid time for landlordism, but not entirely catastrophic. Returning
prosperity in the 1850s was followed by a period of quiescence on the
land issue. In 1859 it was reported that the country was quiet, prices
good, farmers prospering and rents well paid.[3] But Irish landlords
were, in the main, neither efficient nor particularly forward-looking,
and they were chronically impecunious.

CONOLLY'S POLITICS

The changes to Conolly's world that had altered the social fabric far beyond what might have been perceived when he first took office, and his perception of the changes, were reflected in his speeches in the House of Commons. Conolly's involvement in the debates in the House of Commons gave an indication of the typical difficulties landowners of the period were experiencing. As a consequence of his contribution to the debates, his interests and public interventions could be seen.

In the late 1860s, the disestablishment of the Church of Ireland debates exposed the concerns of the Anglican community, Conolly among them, and they were troubled about the threat of how this would affect their positions of influence. In 1869 Conolly spoke on the subject, in a way that encapsulated the fears and concerns of Protestant Ireland. The close connection of the Church of Ireland with the state was seen as an integral part of the Union. Church of Ireland Protestants feared that, if that bulwark fell, the Union itself would be in danger. As it turned out, they were not wrong. Conolly's class also saw disestablishment as a diminution of their local power and prestige, as well as the not-inconsiderable patronage, which would be lost. Disestablishment was enacted in 1869, and the fear by Protestant MPs of 'papist' support for Gladstone to the detriment of the landowning community can be seen clearly during the debates.[4] Disestablishment may have represented a loss of status in one way, but it galvanized the Anglican community into taking a defensive position and made the Church of Ireland much stronger, positioning itself as a more visible symbol of the Protestant ascendancy and as their corporate identity.

Entering the 1870s, Conolly was confronted by an even greater escalation of the challenge to the existing establishment, the perennial question of law and order. He spoke in the debates on the Bill for Peace Preservation in Ireland with concern about agitation, specifically in the Dublin area. During the extended debates on the land-purchase and tenant rights question, he was surprisingly fulsome and generous in his praise for the relationships he held with his tenants, having spent most of his life ... among the tenant farmers of Ireland, always receiving kind and generous treatment from his neighbours ... having received the greatest confidence from his tenants and friends: a confidence almost unmerited on his part and he had no hesitation in saying that he would cheerfully give up some of his rights for the benefit of his country.[5]

In these words, Conolly demonstrates that he was caught up in the forces that were directing Irish politics. On the one hand, he was concerned for his tenants but, on the other, he was worried for himself and his fellow landowners and the loss of their lands and, significantly, their hold on authority.

Throughout the decade from 1870 to 1879, parliamentary debates on Irish matters were concerned with the changing flow of political hierarchy from the old order to the rising nationalist interests. Agrarian unrest was a constant preoccupation of the landlord class throughout the century. Agricultural depression did not fully strike until the late 1870s; earlier, agitation was already on the increase around the country, prompting a coercive response from government. During the 1870s, in the face of that unrest by land agitators and other similar disruptions, Conolly called for the suspension of the *Habeas Corpus* Act.[6] This act ensured that court judgments were the means of imprisoning individuals rather than decisions by private power groups. By removing the act it created an inequality in the treatment of suspects who could be imprisoned without a full jury trial. Conolly approved of this suspension, because he believed that it would 'give the police a reality which they did not then possess, and if they were to be given this power, they could arrest the leaders well known to them across Ireland'.[7] Furthermore, he endorsed the ability of his fellow magistrates to deal with any problems locally rather than with outside intervention. His comment that 'the magistrates and the police would be perfectly capable of maintaining order' reveals his concern for a return to calm in the country.[8] This was also contextualized by the sporadic agricultural agitation in previous decades as well as those that presaged the looming Land Wars.

In the final record of his career, in 1871 Conolly faced what was the beginning of the end to the grand juries' powerful hold on the country. In the bill, on the reform of electoral county boards, it was hoped that the rural population would be given greater power to manage their own affairs, with a resulting revolution in Irish county issues. These far-reaching reforms would pave the way for freer elections and what would eventually become the proto-county councils when the Roman Catholic electorate would take part in greater numbers, although local Protestant landlords and merchants continued to participate in local government.[9] Lord Bandon, for example, was chairman of Bandon Urban District Council. Conolly, in his comments during the debate, while 'not blind to its defects', held that the grand jury system was 'not universally disapproved of in Ireland' and was in fact 'highly appreciated'. He failed to see the implications of a system whose rural representatives were appointed by the sheriff without recourse to open elections. In this final session of his career, he asked 'if the Irish parliamentarians wished to sweep away everything hereditary, an ancient and cherished institution, instead of being improved where necessary [and therefore] ruthlessly destroyed ... in favour of elections, what was that but Republicanism?' He believed that 'the people of Ireland had confidence in the gentry, and he should be glad to help ... to reform and improve the existing system', a system he believed was beneficial to the country. There were some who may not have been pleased to be referred to as republicans, however Isaac Butt (MP for Limerick), himself of an elite Protestant background, was not among them. He stated that he was pleased to be considered a republican because 'the one issue before the house was whether the monstrous anomaly of the grand-jury system should be continued, or whether the people were to be trusted to have a voice in the management of their own affairs'.[10] In 1869 Butt had proposed the idea of Home Rule 'that dominated Irish politics for almost half a century'.[11] Butt's divisive Home Rule Bill would later cause a fundamental cleavage between unionists and nationalists under Parnell. As 'protestant' and 'unionist' began to assume interchangeability, Irish national identity became enmeshed with Roman Catholicism. Ultimately, this would result in alienation.[12]

Conolly died before the fundamental upheaval in Irish politics caused by the rise of Parnell and Gladstone's conversion to the merits of Home Rule. He was the last of his family to participate directly in parliamentary politics, his political position was conservative and, ultimately, unionist; but there is an interesting observation by the *Leinster Express* in his obituary in 1876. They reported that he led those he met in America in 1865 to believe that he supported Home Rule, whereas 'When he crossed the pond and came home [to Britain],

Home Rule stank in his nostrils and disturbed his temper'.[13] The *Leinster Express* opinion of Conolly's position is somewhat creative; in 1865 details of Butt's Home Rule Bill were yet to be developed and would not be forwarded to parliament until 1869. If Conolly had an opinion on the politics of Home Rule, it was, like others at this time, only a theoretical concept and had not achieved any solid political form.

Conolly's political pronouncements were a sort of final struggle to maintain his own and his class's hold on a power that had begun to slip away. While the later material in this book looks at subtler markers of the social network, one can see in the more public and specifically political pronouncements that Conolly made during his life a clear backing for the tangible material processes and governance that maintained ascendency power during his lifetime.

THE SEASON: DUBLIN AND LONDON

The parliamentary season began in October and ran until August, thus concentrating those with political duties in London who were joined by the remainder of society between March and August. Conolly's social network begins in relation to his combined social and political duties. He was frequently in London during the winter season because of his parliamentary responsibilities as the Member of Parliament for Ballyshannon. The elite of society naturally gravitated to London for what was known as 'the season', which roughly corresponded to parliamentary activities but did not formally begin until March/Easter, ending in August. Like other Irish MPs, Conolly availed himself of the round of entertainment available among the society of Irish and English power elites, the majority of whom were also in London in connection with their parliamentary duties. The practice was for politicians and elite families to rent a house for the season if they did not own a London home. In 1830 Colonel Edward Conolly, Thomas's father, took a house in Grosvenor Square. In the 1860s, Conolly took a house at 9 Hanover Square and on another occasion 17 Grafton Street in Mayfair, the fashionable area of London.

A sample of a London season for Conolly can be gleaned from his diaries. In early 1853 with parliament closed – it did not sit from Christmas 1852 until April 1853 – Conolly was in Ireland, but in a series of diary entries he recorded going over to Liverpool in February where he socialized with a friend and went to the races at Birkenhead. A week later, on return to Dublin, he travelled down to Castletown in 'a car, having missed the 7am town train by sleeping soundly in Packet. Round farm & [back] to Dublin by Dog Cart having [been] … at home previously and down to Lifford by night mail'.[14] The following week after meeting the bishop of Derry in Derry he hunted in Dunboyne and then returned to the UK. He remained in London until May when he mentions attending the house for his last speech on Income Tax.[15] In the next extant diary, 1857, parliament sat during February and March and only after it closed did he return to Ireland, having spent the previous months of his stay in London attending myriad social engagements.

These seasonal migrations were a necessity for those attending parliament as MPs but were also required in networking terms for social enrichment, entertainment and political advancement and of course to meet potential marriage partners. Nevertheless, there were those who chose not to travel to London for the season and they congregated in Dublin in what Lady St Helier described as the aristocratic 'Vice-regal entourage … for five or six weeks' of the season.[16] Any events in Dublin Castle and the vice-regal lodge[17] during the season followed closely the type of events at the royal court in London such as levees, drawing-rooms balls and presentations of young women to the viceroy as the queen's representative. Within this relatively short period there was a great deal of dining, theatre going and seasonal balls, some connected with a daughter's coming out, and her presentation at the vice-regal lodge. Those in London were caught in the same whirl of socializing only on a far more lavish and hierarchal level – as the London season was considered substantially more important and protocol more strictly observed. The British parliament functioned partially in parallel with the Irish social season, which began officially at the end of January and ended with the St Patrick's Day Ball in March. Nevertheless, parliamentarians would participate in the season of both countries when they could.

The viceroy – the king's representative in Ireland – held lavish social events at Dublin Castle throughout the Irish season to which the elites were invited. However, strict rules as to who were to be invited were regulated not only by protocol dictated by the court

of St James in London but by a hierarchy largely consisting of the
aristocracy.[18] Dublin Castle operated almost like an elite club to
which only a select few belonged. Burke points out another subtle
division of the ascendancy elite: those invited to the vice-regal lodge,
the viceroy's residence, 'constituted the real elite … the general run
of ascendancy society were entertained … at Dublin Castle'.[19] If
Conolly were a member of this inner circle, being invited to the vice-
regal lodge itself, there is no way of knowing at this time given the
lack of specific references in his diary. However, wider newspaper
reports of the period indicate that he was attending events at Dublin
Castle, both as a single man with his mother and sisters and later with
his wife Sarah Eliza. It does seem unlikely, given his connections, that
he would not be part of that scene.

The *Daily Express* recorded the events of the vice-regal lodge and
Dublin Castle levees, drawing-room balls and dinners and reports
of the 1851 season revealed the families in the highest cohort of
society: Marquis and Lady Drogheda, earl and countess of Desart,
Viscount and Lady Monck, Rt Hon. W.F. Tighe and his wife Lady
Louisa, bishops of Down & Connor and Limerick together with their
wives, Sir Robert Pakenham, Rt Hon. Thomas Conolly and Mrs and
Misses Conolly.[20] These names repeatedly occur as members of elite
clubs, societies and hunt clubs and, in a reflection of the change in
the attitudes to economic endeavour, many are also increasingly seen
as directors of high-profile business ventures such as railways and
major banks. This attendance by Conolly at Dublin Castle would
continue to be recorded in other sample newspapers as well as brief
mentions regarding his travel between Ireland and England in the
social calendar of the *Weekly Irish Times* throughout the 1860s and
1870s. Invitations to Dublin Castle balls given by the viceroy or the
lord lieutenant were seen as a confirmation of high status. 'The pomp
and pageantry associated with the royal court in England was imitated
in Ireland through the office of the lord lieutenant'.[21]

Once the Dublin season was over, the elite families moved their
households across the Irish Sea to catch up with the London season
running from Easter to August. In the 1864 season, Conolly shipped
staff, luggage and horses across to London at a cost of £100. His valet
would arrive later at a further cost of £50.[22]

CONOLLY'S SOCIAL AND SPORTING LIFE

The multitude of places that formed Conolly's world during the parliamentary and social seasons gave a hint of interconnected lives. Between 15 May and 10 August 1857, Conolly recorded countless social commitments in London during the day and evening, both before and after dining, with approximately sixty-four dinner engagements (the diaries can be vague and hard to understand at times). In one week, typically, during the day Conolly rode in Hyde Park, met with friends, lunched at his club or went to the races. In the evening he dined with friends in their homes nearly every night, hosted dinners in the house he had taken for the season and visited the theatre more than once.

Balls, apart from Castle and Court, were organized by high-status women and usually held in their homes during the season in both Dublin and London. For a high-status woman at this time, her 'job was to uphold her husband's position' or, if she was a single woman, her father's or her brother's, if her mother was not in a position to carry out this task. This responsibility was to 'maintain the family's reputation' by doing their utmost to successfully manage the dinner parties that were a key part of the season. For women the purpose of entertaining at home was to 'maintain tradition and class solidarity'.[23] Conolly mentions in his diaries attending balls both in Ireland and in London during the season. In Ireland in March 1853, he wrote of arriving for a ball at Dublin Castle by special train from Moorfield, the country home of the earl of Drogheda near Monasterevin. He reported that fifty-seven sat down to dinner at '7:30 one evening and [it] lasted until 7:30 the next morning'.[24] There were also balls mentioned in the diaries in connection with the hunt meets, organized by the local master and held either in the master's home, usually a country house, or later in the nineteenth century, in large country hotels. Conolly's socializing, after late-night dining with friends, extended to women of the demi-mode in the streets and squares of London. These encounters are repeatedly mentioned throughout the diaries with symbols and comments about these pleasures. This activity would lead to serious consequences for his long-term health.

Conolly's private life is chronicled in his diaries but there is little reflective comment in them; the diaries, largely engagement daybooks, regrettably show little of the private person. It can be argued, however, that by reading between the lines and relying on parallel social histories of the time, the wider lifestyle of Conolly can be deduced and this is their value: to throw light on his own specific place within wider networks. On rare occasions they did contain more detail and revealed more about him as a person. The death of his sister Louisa who tragically drowned in 1853[25] was a rare insight into his emotional landscape. In a series of entries, he described how the news was given to him and how he had to relay this information to his mother and sisters, the journey to Ardgillan in Co. Dublin where her death occurred and, finally, he sadly wrote into the diary part of a poem by Byron[26] that reflected a very palpable grief.[27] There were a further two episodes in his diary that were full of adventure and offered a broader impression of his seemingly spirited personality. An exciting episode occurred in August 1863 when Conolly visited France and described spending time in Paris, with his horses and groom, and how he became entranced with a young woman artist of the demi-mode. He also described his involvement in the French Army manoeuvres at the invitation of Napoleon III and his encounters with the emperor's young son, Napoleon, the Prince Imperial (1856–79). He was very impressed by the military men that he met, among them General Emile Fleury (Grand Equerry to Napoleon III) and Marshal McMahon the duc de Magenta (1808–93), Marshal of France and later the first president of the Third Republic. Of this event, he offered no commentary on the deeper social and political implications. Instead, the entries are full of exuberant exclamation marks and the significance of mixing with such heroic military men.[28] But despite the social entanglements with such exalted persons, what engaged him most in Paris was his horses. He wrote how immensely proud he was of them and that they matched any other horses he encountered.

Later in 1868, on their honeymoon in Paris, Conolly and his new bride Sarah Eliza (née Shaw) had another social encounter with Napoleon III. Not only was it an indication of the level of society they moved in, it was also an indication of Connolly's extravagance.

In an informal challenge the two men competed in the equipage of their horses and carriages but Conolly came out on top because his horses were shod in silver.[29] The fact that a relatively unknown young MP from rural Ireland had an association with the French emperor may speak of Conolly's *savoir faire* and the more relaxed social networks in the nineteenth century, even if these were rare and unusual events. Conolly's eldest son's obituary in 1900 reported that this friendship with Napoleon III even pre-dated their meeting in 1863 at the military manoeuvres. The obituary contained an anecdote about Napoleon III's marriage in 1853 and quotes Conolly: 'I am so old a friend of the emperor that I can take the liberty of making a wedding present'. The same article also reported that later, when he was overthrown, 'Tom Connolly was a good friend to Prince Louis Napoleon following the Franco-Prussian War when he was deposed and living in London'.[30]

ENHANCING CASTLETOWN

In the world of the power elite, 'the building made the individual as much as the individual made the building'.[31] The surroundings of the house and indeed the house itself required regular reinvention to maintain the high level of performance demanded by the individual himself as well as his social status. From the 1850s Conolly was managing projects at Castletown, evident in a deed of covenant with William Cotter, civil engineer, in 1850.[32] In the 1860s he was also involved in a process of maintenance and development, enhancing the park and creating an elaborate gateway to the kitchen garden. The new kitchen in the west wing (fig. 2.3) was also undergoing works from late 1863 through to the following year. It is difficult to ascribe costs to any jobs, however, as only the labourers' pay is given in the daily accounts, namely 'John Mangan attending tradesmen in the kitchen' and 'For 4 weeks running tradesmen are attended in the kitchen'. Similarly, for the material arriving from London, the accounts showed only the cost of collection from nearby Hazelhatch railway station: 'Cases of goods for Kitchen from London x 2'; 'Two collections of cases of china and material for the kitchen wing from London' and '9 dozen 9-inch flooring tiles for the kitchen' which amounted to a cost of only shillings or pence. Some small finishing

2.2 Kitchen Garden gateway, 2017

touches were still occurring in May of 1865: 'White china knobs for kitchen door lock' with the final mention in December of that year that noted the 'kitchen lift frame installed'.[33]

This was not, however, the only project underway during Conolly's building phase in the 1860s. Running parallel with the new kitchen was the enhancement of the Kitchen Garden with the erection of an arch at its entrance (fig. 2.2) that had begun in January 1864: 'Cut stone arch for cart entrance to the garden and lime' whose stone and the lime to make mortar indicating a cost of £1 13s. 1d. but '500 stock bricks for new gateway from garden' were not priced in the account books.

2.3 West-wing kitchen (now restaurant), 2017

It was not only in the Kitchen Garden that work was being done; in the following month, the avenue of lime trees was also being planted: 'Cart to Summerhill for 40 young lime trees for the avenue to the Barn' [Barnhall/Wonderful Barn] where they are still enjoyed today. Soon after in 1866 there was another project commissioning one of the prominent architects of the day Sir Thomas Newenham-

2.4 The Garden House, built *c.*1866 (Shuldham Shaw Collection)

Deane and his partner Benjamin Woodward to design and build a fine garden house, with an extensive greenhouse attached (fig. 2.4). Early in December it was noted that stone for 'new garden house' had been delivered and by July a stove to heat it arrived, 'Edmonston's new stove for new garden house'.[34] In choosing the prestigious firm of Deane & Woodward, which was 'one of the most remarkable and successful practices', for the garden house project, this became a set piece of construction that demonstrated Conolly's high status. They created 'some of the most significant buildings of their time' among them were the quadrangle of Queen's University Cork, the Museum of Natural History in Oxford and, significantly for Conolly, the Kildare Street Club.[35] In employing this architectural firm, Conolly made a deliberate statement about his sophisticated taste and in doing so established a connection not alone with the architects themselves but with other commissioning patrons of similarly high cultural credit. With this garden building, a fairly typical example of high Victorian garden structures, he sought to increase his own cultural credit as well as his imaginary lifeworld. A lifeworld is an intertwining of person and place as a sort of co-produced life, where a grand theatre of objects are variously arranged in space and time relative to the viewer and indeed the creator of the space and place.

These projects were representative of Conolly's ability to spend money on luxury goods demonstrating his conspicuous consumption, that in turn added to his cultural capital as a marker of power. Class and status can be linked in many ways through the ownership of property with astonishing regularity.[36] This is a powerful comment on the way the landowners of the past are viewed. Within the highly regulated societies of the nineteenth century, property owners controlled substantial aspects of their tenants' and employees' lives and that impact on individual lives was considerable. For some, this view lingers into the present. In looking in more detail at the history of Castletown, we see that emerge in a range of ways.

CASTLETOWN HOUSE IN PLACE, SPACE AND TIME

Castletown House represents on one level a physical space: an eighteenth-century house in the landscape of Co. Kildare. On another level, it involves emotional associations tied specifically to the visual impact of the house that embodied its meaning as an identifiable site of wealth and power. In historical terms, it has been of national significance, given that its original owner William Conolly, a native Irishman, had been an influential and powerful eighteenth-century Speaker of the Irish House of Commons. In the heyday of the Protestant ascendancy, the houses of the power elite served as the focus of macro social networking on a vast scale. The house was the very visible hub of networked activity; from gatherings for something as significant as the heir's twenty-first birthday celebration, to wedding parties, to the starting point of an outdoor pursuit such as the arranged hunt meets, associated point-to-point race meetings and shooting parties. As Elizabeth Bowen points out, the creation of the country house was 'purely a social one', to entertain and offer hospitality in the large rooms; this is particularly accurate if one includes social prestige.[37] At a local scale, the more micro-networked elements such as the house and the demesne would have been the location of other leisure activities, such as shooting and fishing, cricket, tennis and croquet where guests stayed for long or short periods.

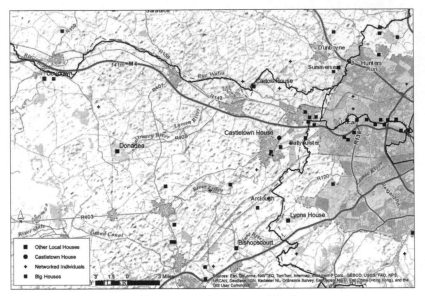

2.5 Houses and demesnes in the vicinity of Castletown, 2017

While impressive on its own, Castletown House was not isolated in its immediate landscape. Other significant houses surrounded it and this first map (fig. 2.5) demonstrates the local network of large and middle-sized houses within a 5-mile radius of Castletown.[38] While not all of the landowners would have been of equal social status, all would have been very aware of each other and would have been networked with each other. Among those of an equal social status, visiting by both men and women to each other's homes would have been a regular occurrence. In the hunting field, men would have known each other through their city-based clubs and both men and women through local and social acquaintances. For women, meeting in private homes, at hunt meets, point to points and balls, as well as attendance at church, would have reinforced the family network on a micro level. Other houses on this map were owned by individuals that Conolly was acquainted with: the Clements at Kiladoon was the closest house, Leixlip Castle was rented to the Cavendishes, married to a distant family member, the Kennedys were at Enfield, a name that frequently recurs in his diary, Cloncurry was at Lyons, a family member; and at Kill, Bishopscourt was owned by the earl of Clonmell.

The duke of Leinster, who lived nearby at Carton estate, is a name that one would expect to see in the diaries, but Conolly mentions him and Carton only briefly in his 1853 diary. Nevertheless, not only did their social lives overlap, but their lands were also interlinked; the great eighteenth-century obelisk erected by Kathleen Conolly and known as Conolly's Folly was built on lands owned by the FitzGeralds. This implies a deep connection between the two families and a mutual agreement on creating statements of control of the landscape. The duke and his family had high levels of cultural capital and were members of both the KSC and the Kildare Hunt and, for that reason alone, they would have been known to Conolly. The close relationship between the two families in the eighteenth century, however, does not appear to have survived as strongly in the nineteenth. Although the name of the duke's brother Lord Otho FitzGerald appears in the newspapers as attending functions at Castletown and hunt meets, with the exception of listing him as a dinner-party guest, no other mention of him appears in the diaries. The other possibility, which cannot be confirmed, is that the connection was so close that, like the passing mention of his mother and sisters in the diaries, it was not necessary to note the relationship. Landowners whose property adjoined Castletown purchased land and property in the 1920s when it came up for sale; Lord Dease, resident at Oakley Park, Celbridge, bought the townland of Kildrought, a section of the demesne itself, as well as parts of Celbridge town, and Leixlip town and castle.

By the nineteenth century, the role of the big house as an overarching power base had diminished. Nevertheless, across Ireland, great families like the Conollys, living in their large houses, acted as powerful symbols of the old order to the wider population. While Conolly had never reached the lofty heights of the Speaker's status, given that his role as MP for Ballyshannon was of minor importance nationally, he was nevertheless a visible agent within the parameters of Castletown. He was also highly visible in two other nodal settings: his second home Cliff in Donegal, and the other significant spatial node in his lifeworld, the British House of Commons. From a social networking perspective, it was the interactions and interplay between these three nodal points that was of foundational importance to the development of that network.

Given the reduced power of Thomas Conolly, the power impact of Castletown House and its surrounding parkland in the context of the wider society in the nineteenth century was, at first glance, largely local, particularly as he employed thirty people. The household accounts clearly indicate there was an outdoor staff of around twenty, but the number of indoor staff is not entirely clear. Generally, in large country houses there would have been between ten and fifty indoor staff but in the case of Castletown it was more likely to have been closer to the lower figure. The house, until the 1890s, remained the home to one single family and its place as part of a spatial network of other houses and their owners in proximity was through formal and informal relationships.

In the present, if Castletown seems little changed in its material form, the character of the house has altered considerably. The power previously vested in it is now only an anecdote and what imaginative power remains is primarily in connection to heritage tourism. The contemporary controlling bodies, the Castletown Foundation and the Office of Public Works, have sustained the link to culture by offering musical events, art exhibitions and talks as well as food and craft markets. On one level, it is now a space that has perhaps a greater national significance than previously, drawing visitors to Castletown via its cultural and heritage status. The cultural position expanded to another level in 2010 when it received museum accreditation, drawing in cultural tourists from Europe and North America and further afield. Its older political power has been replaced, but its echoes have been commodified in part because of the social cultural past.

THE AMERICAN ADVENTURE: CONOLLY AS A CONFLICT TOURIST

In the 1860s, despite Conolly's level of social connectivity, ever-present in the Conolly family story were their financial problems. Inherited debts, jointures and obligations were not his fault; but these were not helped by his own excessive lifestyle. These combined financial difficulties set Conolly on a very significant path in his already thrill-seeking life when he began an American adventure at the end of 1864. His diary of November that year showed that for someone who was an elected member of the government he had planned a risky and questionable enterprise. The proposed plan was, with others, to finance a boat to run the Yankee blockade then in place in the waters off the southern Confederate States during the American Civil War.[39] The first indication comes in November 1864 from his distant cousin Emily Barton who wrote to him 'I am so glad to hear you are one of us'. Although the details are sketchy, it seems that John Palliser, a member of the Royal Geographical Society, together with 'Mr Tottenham of Ballycurry, Lord Charlemont, Colonel [William Dixon] Bushe, Sir B. Chapman and Colonel MacNamara and lots of others that you know' are already involved. She asks '... have you seen Palliser and what are you going to do?'[40] Palliser was a Waterford man and was distantly related to Conolly and Barton and probably in a similar tight financial situation. Someone who could be described as an 'explorer', he had been the leader of the British North American Exploring Expedition, which between 1857 and 1861 surveyed the boundary between British North America and the United States, from Lake Superior to the coast of the Pacific Ocean. He had also been to the southern United States in 1862 just as the blockade by the United States Navy was put in place during the American Civil War in the waters off the southern Confederate States. This mysterious journey is thought by some to have been at the behest of certain Caribbean islands and the Confederate States but there is no evidence he was a spy.[41]

The proposed plan was to finance the ship *Emily* to run the Union blockade. The *Emily* was the commodity and any cargo she might be carrying was incidental. She was a sleek paddle steamer of 220 feet, that could make twenty knots in fair weather. She may also have had a cargo of marine engines because, according to N.D. Lankford's research, Palliser and the Confederate navy had been discussing this early in the previous year.[42]

Only ten days after receiving Barton's letter, on 26 November Conolly was ready to set off on his journey and he articulated his financial concerns on paper. In his diary he described sitting in the morning light at Summerhill with his sister Harry (Henrietta) who shared her cup of coffee with him. He wrote that he wanted 'to strike off the fetters of home associations and embark ourselves and our fortunes in the ship *Emily*'. If he had not heard of the project before 6 November this was a very hasty decision to get involved in on the spur of the moment and indicates the type of risk-taker he was. He had received advice from 'officious friends' to abandon the enterprise but he ignored them. In the diary there is a document dated July 1864 describing the costs of the proposed journey but there is no telling when or where he got this summary; it is not in his handwriting.

Conolly's diary entry of 26 November 1865 reads 'Dear old Palliser is waiting at the Inn at Waterford'. After meeting, they separated, with Palliser going to London while Conolly made his way to Cardiff, the destination of the *Emily*, which had been built on the Clyde estuary. Soon after reaching Cardiff he wrote: 'Ship has arrived! Go aboard and shake hands with Captain ... Telegram to Prichard Walker to arrange money oh dear!' Later, providing evidence of the origins of the enterprise, he wrote that Palliser was 'the author and founder of our expedition'.[43]

Conolly had expressed worries and hopes concerning his finances and the economic advantage to the voyage, before and after meeting Palliser. Nevertheless, the early entries revealed the motivations, apart from the financial reward, for the journey. In reading his diary, we find he felt 'an intense desire for adventure and this one is particularly hallowed by the great Cause of the South'. This, of course, is especially interesting because the 'great cause of the south' was in part the retention of slavery. Furthermore, he indicated that 'his life had been wasted in inaction' and chaffed at the 'responsibility being the master of Castletown'. Inaction is not a word that comes to mind and one wonders why he did not join the army if he felt he needed action in his life; every male member of his extended Pakenham family had joined up, but he had not. This is a question we are unlikely to have an answer to. Finally, he complained that being the owner of property requires so much reliance on countless others he finds it overwhelming. Following these early passages, his difficulties, emotional or financial, were not referred to again.

Things did not go well on the voyage and in late December after eight days at sea the ship was storm-damaged.[44] Sailing in December might not have been a wise decision. The ship just managed to reach Madeira safely but not without Conolly suffering what he described in his diary as a culinary disaster in the galley when the rolling ship threw him on to a pot of soup and, capping it off, a shelf collapsed and condiments and molasses covered his hair. Arriving at Funchal, the capital of Madeira, with which he appears to have been familiar, he

2.6 Thomas Conolly, *c.*1865, by William Osborne (1823–1901)

met old friends and some cousins. The damage to the ship prompted a naval board inquiry and a survey that concluded she was not capable of crossing the Atlantic without repairs. At this point, Captain Foster with Palliser and Robert McDowell took the *Emily* to Cadiz in Spain for repairs and here the *Emily* and these men disappear from the diaries.

At this juncture, although the ship and possible cargo were on hold, Conolly and Bushe decide to continue the adventure, hoping that after repairs the *Emily* would be able to travel to meet them in Nassau. After a period of merrymaking in Madeira, early in the new year the two men took passage on the ship *Florence* heading for Bermuda, where they arrived on 13 January.

St George Harbour, Bermuda, is described as a 'robbers' den' of pubs, brothels and all manner of shady characters. And, in a letter to his sister, he wrote of St George's that only 'Hogarth could possibly produce a convincing portrait of the town'. Despite this observation, or possibly because of it, they jumped right into the mayhem and

spent twelve days enjoying themselves before continuing in the
Florence to the Bahamas. While waiting in Nassau, it must have been
obvious to the two men that the *Emily* was not going to meet them
to make the run to Richmond. They opted instead to continue with
the *Florence* as it attempted to run the blockade on 2 February. After
a collision at sea with another blockader, they were forced back to
Nassau. By the end of the month, however, they took passage on *The
Owl*, the last blockade-runner on the Carolina coast. Conolly and
Bushe with two Americans were at last able to make landfall, but the
landing boat was tossed by the breakers, which threw their luggage
into the water. After rescuing both the boat and their luggage they
reached the town of Shallotte in the pouring rain and hid their bags
under an upturned boat. Sending the pilot with Bushe back to *The
Owl* for rifles, Conolly was housed by the Pigott family who dried
his clothing and fed him while he waited for Bushe. But Bushe did
not return, instead sailing back to Nassau on *The Owl* and 'chose a less
hazardous route to New York'.[45]

The following day, Conolly, accompanied by the two American
travellers William A. Selden and W.S. Sterrett, with John Pigott and
his horse and cart carrying the luggage, set off to the nearest ferry
40km away. Taking care to avoid the Yankee lines, they travelled with
some difficulty through the swamps and woods of North Carolina.
Lankford estimates that Conolly was one of the last foreign visitors
to see the dying days of the Confederacy.[46]

It took them nine days to battle their way through the hinterland on
their way to Raleigh, passing through the small town of Fayetteville
to obtain the travel passes necessary for safe conduct through the
Confederacy. On the way, Conolly recorded staying at small plantations
and farms for the night and meeting people whose sons were off
fighting. As they travelled, there were signs of war all around as well as
Yankee prisoners and a lot of movement by troops and civilians trying
to transport goods out of the way of Sherman's advance.

Throughout the entire three months, Conolly speaks of food in
the diary entries; fine food, hearty breakfasts, and no food. Any hotels
he stayed at were full of soldiers where the talk of the different types
of side arms and rifles everyone carried was incessant. And wherever
Conolly went there were other Irishmen wanting to meet him, have a
drink and talk of home.

In every grand house he visited there was plenty to eat and drink. Contrary to the assumption one makes about the difficulties faced in the dying days of the Civil War, the larders of the wealthy in their fashionable homes and farmhouses were evidently not as empty as one supposed. One must also take into account a desire to put their best foot forward for Conolly's presence. On the other hand, the quality of food at one inn was so poor he complained to the woman who owned the establishment; at this her husband pulled a gun and threatened him. Conolly's two American companions had to step in to calm the situation.

Finally arriving safely in Raleigh, with his luggage, he walked about and described in his diary how well-built the town was and how beautifully situated, topped by a capitol building set about with Doric columns. His two American companions, Selden and Sterrett, introduced him to all and sundry including, surprisingly, the *Times* correspondent covering the war, Francis Lawley, a former MP and private secretary to William Gladstone, and Mr Visitelli, a correspondent of the *Illustrated London News*. He also met State Governor Zebulon Vance at the capitol, where he was one of the most effective southern-state leaders going about his wartime duties. Conolly was invited by Vance to ride in his carriage part of the way to Richmond, and charged Major General Wilcox with seeing him safely to his destination.

Here, Conolly can be seen as a tourist. He certainly had the ability to organize a party: 'I arrange a banjo band and whiskey and invite the wounded officers to my room for dancing, singing and negro music until 1'. After partying until 1am he was up again at 2.30am to catch the train. He found that 'soldiers and prisoners in all manner of garb and motley troops fill the train, with women and children crying'. He wrote that he and the men pass a bottle of spirits around. Eventually finding a corner in the guard's car, he fell asleep on the luggage.

On 7 March he at last arrived in Richmond. The local paper had foretold of his coming when they had previously encountered him in Fayetteville. After meeting Senator James Mason, he observed that

> Richmond was wretched with the shops empty and the streets filled with people ranging from rowdies, rustics, intoxicated, mad, moody, sparkling and groups of mud-splattered cavalry.

There are uniforms of every variety interspersed with smart officers and neat battle-hardened veterans and mud, mud, mud everywhere.

Being the romantic he was, Conolly wrote that the situation of the tree-lined city is magnificent on a bend in the James River. At his large, miserably furnished hotel, the *Ballard House*, having only beds and a few broken chairs, such was inflation that drinking glasses cost $25 each and a bottle of brandy was $60.

Looming over the visit was the war still raging throughout the southern states. From 15 November until 21 December 1864, Union General William T. Sherman led some sixty thousand soldiers on a 285-mile march from Atlanta to Savannah, Georgia. The purpose of Sherman's 'March to the Sea' was to frighten Georgia's civilian population into abandoning the Confederate cause. Sherman's soldiers did not destroy any of the towns in their path, but they stole food and livestock and burned the houses and barns of people who tried to fight back. The Yankees were 'not only fighting hostile armies, but a hostile people', Sherman explained; as a result, they needed to 'make old and young, rich and poor, feel the hard hand of war'.[47]

Throughout Conolly's stay in Richmond, the dining with cocktails in abundance and dancing continued with pretty girls from Savannah, Wilmington, Charleston and Columbia who had fled from Sherman's advance. Despite, or perhaps regardless of, Sherman coming inexorably closer, an impromptu dance was organized with three Confederate generals in attendance and a congressman as well as plenty of other officers. Malvina Gist wrote in her memoirs 'Oh yes, we know Mr Conolly an Irish MP and southern sympathizer. He seems to have plenty of money and lives at the hotel in great style for war times'.

At church in Richmond, he met Jefferson Davis, president of the Confederacy, and in the coming weeks would spend time with him shortly before the city was overrun. The next day after a breakfast party he accompanied General Wilcox to the senate to meet Davis, his staff, other politicians and army personnel. At this time, he met the head of the secret service, Chief Communications Officer William Norris, who he described as a 'crafty fellow with a horrid squint'.

Close to the city, the lines of defence were held by Lieutenant General James Longstreet (1821–1904), one of the foremost Confederate generals and principal subordinate to Robert E. Lee. Longstreet's corps consisted of forty thousand men and Conolly, in company with Longstreet, viewed their defences and forts, which communicated by telegraph with Lee at his Edgehill headquarters some distance away at Petersburg.

That night he visited President Davis, his talkative and bitter wife and his family, discussing the war for two hours.

> Davis is a remarkable man! His quiet manner and ready easy conversation ... mask a man of extraordinary determination. He seems to be entirely impressed with the awful destinies he is wielding and yet is never despondent and never says a word against those southern scoundrels who continually carp against him.

On 15 March he travelled to the front lines at Petersburg south-east of Richmond in the company of General C.M. Wilcox to view the preparations for the coming battle. On arrival in Petersburg, he gave his usual travelogue: 'the church steeple has a hole in it and all the houses show evidence of shelling'; he also described lunch, complaining of just the one bottle of claret available. More positively, Wilcox's quarters were in a 'smiling farmhouse in a grove of trees almost idyllic'.

The next day they visited General Lee, the general in charge of the army of northern Virginia and soon to become the chief general of the Southern Confederacy. Lee was

> the idol of his soldiers and the hope of his country. The handsomest man in all that constitutes the real dignity of man that I ever saw ... with an easy courteous manner, one of the most prepossessing figures that ever bore the weight of command or led the fortunes of a nation.

Touring the camp and the Confederate front lines, he observed some 200–300 yards away the Federal camp 'with a huge Yankee ensign waving in the breeze'. After a meal containing the largest turkey he had ever seen and a vintage Madeira, Lee showed Conolly a map of the defences of Richmond – ones that would soon prove inadequate. Later on, back in Richmond, after church he would meet Lee's family. Lodging in the town of Petersburg there were the usual dancing and singing of patriotic songs with pretty ladies. Despite all the war preparations, he was recording dinners, tea parties, buggy rides and walks with the ladies; all very civilized and most curious under the circumstances.

The diary does not indicate if he felt under any immediate threat but on 22 March Conolly began to think about the arrangements for moving on to New York via Fredericksburg some distance further north. To this end, he took $50 in Confederate money out of the bank, which is very little considering that by the final days of the war inflation had reached an incredible 9,000 per cent.[48]

Nevertheless, on 25 March he was still in Richmond when he was taken 12km down the James in an ironclad gunboat named the *Torpedo*. This was to see the Confederate fleet anchored downstream below fortifications at Drewry's Bluff. Here he was given a tour by Admiral Raphael Semmes. Conolly was impressed by the order and correctness of the ships and their crews. Although Semmes declared in the wardroom drinks party that 'the Confederacy could and would fight it out to success', he would soon find that the navy was as demoralized as the army.

Even though he had declared his intention to make his way to Fredericksburg, by 29 March Conolly was still travelling between the front lines in Petersburg and Richmond, socializing with 'the lovely ladies' and meeting Lee once again, this time at his headquarters in Edgehill, where it was apparent that the Confederate Army were on the verge of action.

Back in Petersburg on 30 March he viewed a skirmish as it raged before him and where up to five hundred wounded were brought back to the rear. Conolly does not flinch from the battle scenes and reported the 'pickets firing merrily'; 'merrily' perhaps not a word one would expect under these circumstances. After this small skirmish, Conolly offered his services for any coming battle activities and it was agreed that he was welcome to take part but, leaving Petersburg soon after, he did not return to fulfil this invitation. The following day back in Richmond he paid his hotel bill and planned a picnic with several of the ladies of his acquaintance. Not surprisingly, however, this was impossible because of the unsafe conditions on the James; instead, they held a cotillion at the hotel.

That weekend, Conolly was as usual visiting and partying and spent time with Lieutenant General Longstreet and his ADC Thomas Goree going over the maps of the prepared battle lines, and later, after cocktails, they dined together. But after church on Sunday 2 April the first indication that things are not well began to filter in. Longstreet's lines had been breached and word came from Lee that Richmond was to be evacuated. Writing up his diary several days later about his last night in the city, it appears that he was asked by Mrs Enders and her daughters if he would stay the night with them because they 'dreaded those terrible enemies' and the 'poor girls fling themselves down on their sofas and chairs and weep and sob until their hearts seem breaking'. On the morning of 3 April the women finally went to bed at 4am, but he stayed up watching: 'then there is the death knell of Richmond' with the 'shock of the exploding magazine followed by another and another'.

Conolly was apparently at some point outside in the thick of it because he described that the street was 'filled with ragamuffins and Negros running and hurrying about'. Looting was occurring, 'with men and women bustling about with more than they can carry'. The mills were on fire by then too and the crowds were rushing in to carry out the flour. Pushing and elbowing his way back to the Enders to say goodbye, he returned to his hotel hearing the shouts of the approaching Yankee soldiers. The Union Army under Ulysses S. Grant was converging on the city when Lee gave the order for the Confederate troops to withdraw. The retreating soldiers were under orders to set fire to bridges, the armoury and warehouses full of supplies as they left. The fire in the largely abandoned city spread out of control, reaching to the very edge of Capitol Square mostly unchecked. The conflagration was not completely extinguished until the mayor and other civilians went to the Union lines east of Richmond and surrendered the city the next day. Grant pursued Lee and he surrendered a week later.

On 3 April Conolly was on the road with all of the other refugees including Confederate officers heading west to Lynchburg. Early in the journey he waved off the *Times* correspondent Lawley as he planned to follow Lee and the remnants of the Confederate Army as they fled to nearby Appomattox where Lee later surrendered. Eventually travelling north, they found evidence everywhere of Sheridan's raiding party, burning houses with dead horses rotting in the heat. And whether they were true or not, he gave anecdotal reports of atrocities inflicted by the Union Army on southern supporters. He continued with his horse barely able to carry him in company with 'a pretty lady in a wagon with her negro servants and children. She was trying to reach her husband, an officer under Lee, at Culpepper', north-west of Fredericksburg. By now, in nearly every diary entry, he wrote about giving away his personal items in exchange for food and shelter.

Going further north, closer to Bowling Green, he wrote of the banter and companionship of his fellow travellers. This included Capt. John Tayloe V of the 9th Virginia Cavalry, with whom he was compelled to share a bed in various houses along the way. Just before Bowling Green, his horse collapsed but they found shelter with 'Mrs Burress who gave us some excellent homemade wine and her table was covered with rustic profusion despite the Yankees having taken a large amount of her stock and provisions'. He left her with his ivory brushes bearing the Conolly crest. Finally reaching Bowling Green, they saw more evidence of the army, with burnt houses, and moved quickly to Port Royal some 70–80km from Richmond, where they again shared lodging, coffee and corn bread in another rustic establishment run by Mrs Gibbs, to whom he promised a calico dress.

On 6 April they finally reached Chatterton, Tayloe's home and his 'dear little children Lucy Kate and Minnie', in a more peaceful area, around 115km from Richmond and 25km from Port Royal. Here, with the Potomac River as backdrop, Conolly enjoyed 'the perfect peace of this beautiful situation … after the troubles and agonies and toil of warfare out of which we have emerged. Truly it seems like an enchantment'. As a gift to Tayloe, 'I gave him my Russian chain of gold and platinum in token of his valued friendship and General Lee and his noble army'. Tayloe was a member of one of the first families of America, having come over from England in 1640.

On 8 April Conolly was off again on his northward journey with a letter from Tayloe to Capt. Thomas Conrad the notorious Confederate spy whom he described meeting: 'Wearing a black frock coat, clasped belt and pistols, boots and spurs and a black slough hat with a feather, Captain Conrad tied up his horse at the rack'. Conrad, who would later become the president of Virginia Agricultural and Medical School, wrote extensively about his wartime experiences and his book published in 1904 illustrates him as Conolly so wonderfully described.[49]

Conrad arranged to meet Conolly that night at 9pm, but he failed to turn up and, two hours later, with some difficulty, Conolly tracked him down in bed asleep. Undaunted, Conolly bunked down with his crew, all in the same room. The next morning after breakfast at 6am, with 'excellent homemade food and negro servants' to help the hostess Mrs Jeter, Conrad left to preach a sermon at a nearby church. Another arrangement was made for 10pm that night and, collecting his luggage, Conolly headed to the rendezvous but Conrad would not appear until 10.30, 'armed to the teeth'. They 'slip out and row at a rattling pace' across the Potomac River for Maryland on the opposite shore, but 'leaving him to wade some 50 metres on to the bank ... with the luggage'. After paying $450, apparently the last of his Confederate money, he lodged with a family and after breakfast headed off to find another boat to take him to Washington.

He found a Capt. Spalding who was heading for Baltimore but, without any money, Conolly had to work as crew for his passage. Three hours of work allowed him, as he wrote, to 'bunk with the rats, rats and more rats and a negro in the bunk under me' but most importantly to be fed.

They travelled down the Potomac, 'a splendid river ... beautifully wooded on both sides with beautiful bays garnished with trim fishing stations'. Government ships passed and repassed, carrying soldiers, prisoners, ammunition and stores for the Union Army in the Richmond area. He was very impressed with a battleship that he saw, better than any of Semmes' fleet at Fredericksburg, of some three hundred feet in length with huge guns. By 14 April, eleven days after leaving Richmond in flames, he was safely in Baltimore and had, through pure luck, escaped injury. On that same evening, President Lincoln was assassinated in Washington DC by the Confederate sympathizer John Wilkes Booth.

The trip of three months, in the final weeks, even days, of the Civil War, entailed meeting many of the historic figures whose names we are familiar with today. Memoirs of the period serve to provide us with a portrait of Conolly's personality, which ranged from a description of his eccentricities with regard to dress and the vivacity and wit of his social discourse. Though many people were puzzled as to why Conolly would have come to the southern United States during an especially crucial moment of the war, they were captivated by him, which helped to mitigate any objections to his presence.[50] It was unlikely that Conolly had any realistic perception as to what risks he was taking or how dangerous were the waters he was sailing into both politically and physically.[51] From the time he left England on the *Emily* in November 1864 until he returned six months later in May 1865, he experienced many life-threatening events.

What was remarkable about the adventure, however, is how Conolly unwittingly fell in with those whom Lankford calls 'some of the sharpest characters of the Confederacy'. He seemed effortlessly to be in the right place at the right time, meeting Jefferson Davis and Robert E. Lee, who were both willing to spend quality time with him. This speaks of his winning personality, and Major General Wilcox described him as 'a genial and warm-hearted stranger' who 'had all the vivacity, and much of the wit and humor peculiar to his race'. And Lee's friend Mrs Pryor found to her surprise that 'the MP proved a most agreeable guest, a fine-looking Irish gentleman with an irresistibly humorous and cherry fund of talk'. It would appear that Conolly did not act legally when he dipped his toe into the business of profiteering when signing up to the *Emily* project. Leaving behind polite society, he mixed with some very hard men: McNamara on board the *Emily*, Maffit, the blockade-running captain of *The Owl*, and Sterrett, his comrade on a part of the journey. At its end in New York, he encountered a gun-runner, and later, on his escape from Richmond with John Tayloe, he was introduced to the 'colourful desperado' Thomas N. Conrad, the most successful Confederate spy who was arrested soon after Conolly reached safety. Even Spalding, the captain of his transport to Baltimore, who Conolly may have realized was a smuggler, was also a Confederate spy. Conolly was fortunate not to remain in their company for too long in the fluid nature of post-war confusion and sporadic conflict. The diaries do not hint at any awareness of any desperate schemes of the Confederacy operating around him. Instead, Conolly was perpetually in denial that the south would inevitably lose or that their manifestos were skewed. The diaries show his innate frivolity and his lack of vision. One wonders what kind of representative he actually was for his Ballyshannon constituents.

The last month of entries in his diaries in America do not reflect on either his lucky escape or the consequences of the war. After Baltimore, he travelled down to Washington DC purely as a tourist and back up to Philadelphia, where he wrote that the city was in full mourning garb for Lincoln's funeral, and then on to New York. Incredibly, his diary in this period is taken up with a commentary on his near stalking of a young woman, Miss Lena Peters. He seems to visit her constantly, travelling back and forth from New York, and parties at Delmonico's, to Philadelphia hoping to convince her, and her family, to accept him as husband material. They resist his advances and eventually he gave up and flirted his way back to England on the ship *Scotia*. But there was one more near miss: the *Scotia* nudged an iceberg while on its Atlantic crossing but slipped away unscathed.

As to the *Emily* scheme, this ship had been identified as early as December 1864 as a possible blockade runner by the 'United States vice-consul at Glasgow', but the State Department was not immediately aware that the 'wealthy MP' who was involved was to be identified as Conolly.[52] Before his return to the United Kingdom by regular steamship, he was apparently unaware of any threat, sailing for home via Liverpool to take up his political career. Once Conolly had been identified by the federal authorities, there was some attempt to catch up with him before he left America, but the investigation languished until Thomas H. Dudley, the Liverpool consul, 'concluded [...] in a report to Washington' that Conolly had returned to the United Kingdom.[53]

The only serious outcome of the adventure for Conolly appeared to have been financial and, on his return to Ireland, he was forced to sell some of the Castletown lands to avert financial problems.[54] In the following year, just over one thousand acres in Co. Roscommon and other lands in Offaly were advertised for sale, lands originally bought by the Speaker in the early eighteenth century.[55] The family's substantial landholdings in Donegal, totalling 68,633 acres (although with a valuation of only £9,163), were also beginning to be disposed of to settle Conolly's debts. In 1869 the lands close to the town of

Bundoran were sold, which was then rising in status to become a
seaside resort. He refused the first offer of £45,000 from Lord Lifford:
'Conolly was not prepared to take a half-penny under £60,000'.[56] The
Ballyshannon estates bought by the Speaker in 1718 were subsequently
put on the market in 1872. Despite many sales of land during and
after Conolly's lifetime, the *Weekly Irish Times* 'special correspondent'
described the estates in Donegal in 1881 as being the finest in the
north-west. This may have been true in terms of total acreage, as
Conolly was second in the list of Donegal landowners. But 'the two
Donegal properties were very different', one having development
potential (in the south of the county) and the other in the 'bleak lands
of west Donegal'.[57] Again, the role of landholding and its value as an
asset were also part of a wider relational power that was becoming
increasingly challenged in Conolly's lifetime. While some of those
challenges were undoubtedly of his own making, they also reflected
wider upheavals in landownership that affected the position of the
ascendency elite. With the modest wealth at his disposal, Thomas
Conolly carried out some new work and refurbishment at Castletown
House. In this, he was not untypical – many owners of great houses
(and Castletown was a 'Great House', not merely a 'Big House')
were literally 'life tenants' under entails and mortgages, and thus had
little control over their holdings.[58] Although documentary evidence
is limited, his contribution assured that the fabric of the house and
its legacy were sustained for the benefit of his grandchildren and,
ultimately, if not intentionally, for the Irish people.

MARRIAGE AND LATER YEARS

When Conolly finally married he was 45. One cannot be sure what
the delay on Conolly's part was, but there are several possibilities.
First, he was hoping to have a better financial base from which
to offer marriage; secondly, he was too carefree to wish to marry
and third he was waiting for the right woman to come along. The
'right woman' was crucial. Marriages were, after birth connections,
perhaps the most significant associations one could make that acted
as both glue and lubricant in the creation and maintenance of social
networks. Families created alliances that combined a number of areas:
first, based on land and both the retention and consolidation of the

2.7 Sarah Eliza Shaw, *c.*1868, by William Osborne (1823–1901)

landholdings; secondly, through dynastic considerations, it was vital to have an heir, preferably a son, and thirdly, money. A fourth might be the political or social capital that either the bride or the groom could offer. Marrying for love was beginning to be popular for all classes in the nineteenth century, but realistically the higher up the social ladder one was positioned the less likely this was to happen without some degree of control. Once married, a woman, through her family contacts, could bring to the husband other grander social or financial advantages. Marriages for political reasons advanced the groom to parliamentary positions or into appointments only lightly based on merit. Through the financial capacity of the bride's parents, the dowry became the platform from which to develop a larger land portfolio to provide a greater income.

Preferably, she would be from the same social group, Protestant, young enough to produce an heir and, finally and probably most importantly, able to bring money into the union. The financial situation for the Conolly family, and indeed many of the aristocratic and gentry families at the time, was fraught to say the least. The sensible and the largely acceptable thing to do to rectify this was for many elite families to 'marry well' and, while this may seem rather calculating, this is what Conolly set about doing.[59] The advantageous marriage that he entered into in 1868 ticked all the boxes. Thomas at some stage met and courted Miss Sarah Eliza Shaw (1846–1921), whose family lived at Temple Mills in Celbridge.

At just 21, Sarah was twenty-three years younger than Thomas, but her youth and no doubt her dowry formed an attractive combination. All we know are anecdotal stories that the 'lowly' social standing of the bride shocked many of his contemporaries who considered she was 'beneath him'. By looking at the Shaw family history to consider this opinion, it would appear they were far from being beneath him. It is safe to assume the Shaw family was upper-middle-class but not aristocratic. Her aunt was married to Viscount Montmorres and her grandfather was the chancellor of what would soon become Queen's University Belfast. Admittedly, the father of the bride Joseph Shaw was 'in trade'. He was a very wealthy miller, however, whose successful business interests were in Celbridge, where, with his brother, he owned the large mill complex whose buildings remain today. They mixed in high social circles and took a house for the summer seasons in the up-and-coming fashionable seaside town of Bray, so perhaps the 'not good enough' comments were simply mean-spirited.

Although the dowry paid to Thomas was not specified in the detail of the fourteen-page marriage settlement, subsequently it became known that the sum was £10,000.[60] This settlement, if the reports in contemporary memoirs are anything to go by, Conolly spent with alacrity.[61] Although his spending may have been extravagant, he had settled on Sarah Eliza £3,000 per annum based on the annuities from the Kildare estates.[62] In return, Conolly assigned the rights of lands he possessed around Castletown, Celbridge, Leixlip and Straffan, including the land in Donegal, to the earl of Bective and Charles Wolfe Shaw to hold in trust. The earl was Conolly's cousin and Shaw was a close friend of the family, but not a relation.

AN AUTUMN WEDDING

The wedding of Thomas and Sarah Eliza was a spectacle, part of a demonstration of the power of the legitimate authority in the country. Spectacles made statements on how society should be and how it should act in given situations. These events were gazed upon by the general public and largely accepted as the norm for certain elite groups. Semi-private events such as the wedding were fleetingly observed and marvelled at by the public and reported fulsomely in national newspapers.

On 6 September 1868, the marriage of Thomas Conolly of Castletown to Miss Sarah Eliza Shaw of Celbridge occurred in Christ Church, Bray, newly built around that time. The wedding was reported in the newspapers,[63] which were well aware that circulation was dependant on articles about familiar people in the small population of Ireland. Typically, reports of the period gave more details of private events than one would find in today's newspapers. The equivalent for the present might be popular culture magazines such as Tatler, Town and Country or Hello.

The newspapers reported that the wedding party and their 'troops of friends' assembled at the International Hotel in Bray, which was decorated with flags and evergreen. At eleven o'clock the bride, accompanied by her parents and her grandfather Dr P.S. Henry, president of Belfast College, travelled from her parents' summer home at Marine Terrace in Bray to the new church. They rode in a carriage pulled by four white horses, accompanied by outriders in blue wearing wedding favours. Lining the street in Bray were approximately 1,200 people, who viewed the bride as she passed. The Leinster Express described Sarah Eliza as 'very interesting and about twenty' and went on to give an account of her dress and white Brussels lace veil with a simple crown of orange blossoms and ivy leaves. This white and lace fashion had been established with Queen Victoria's wedding dress and has been followed since that time. Her grandfather gave her away and the best man was the Hon. Charles Ponsonby, Thomas's first cousin (his mother was a Ponsonby). Sixteen young ladies acted as bridesmaids, all dressed in white satin with pink and blue ribbons.[64]

In the newspaper reports, two things of significance can be seen: the reporter or the paper is anxious to be complimentary about the event and the family's upper-middle-class and aristocratic connections are spotlighted. Bray was at this time a very fashionable seaside town popular with the upper classes and the location would have added to the prestige and status of the wedding. The Shaw family rented 1 Marine Terrace for six weeks during the summer months as they had done for several years, and they would have been known to the local people who were interested enough to come out to watch. The crowd assembled in the town and church were offered a display of significant spectacle: the splendid bridal carriage and, although not mentioned by the reporters, the arrival of the sixteen bridesmaids in their various carriages and the many wedding guests, which would have added to the excitement. The service itself was conducted by the bishop of Derry, William Alexander, and assisted by other clergy. Presumably, the bishop of Derry was chosen because Conolly's constituency was within the diocese.

After the wedding the company adjourned to the gardens of the Royal Marine Hotel where Mr William Lawrence of Sackville Street took several views of the party.[65] This was followed by the reception at the International Hotel, where a sumptuous dejeuner was provided for 230 invitees. Following this there were the traditional toasts proposed by the best man, Mr Ponsonby, Prof. Henry and Colonel Conolly, Thomas's brother. The bridegroom, Joseph Shaw, and Lord Longford, the groom's cousin, then responded to the toasts. At the conclusion of the meal, a five-foot six-inch wedding cake, by Mrs Mitchell of 10 Grafton Street, decorated with real flowers, was served. The bride and bridegroom departed by 5.30pm train for the Royal FitzWilliam Hotel, Rathdrum, in the Vale of Avoca, where they remained for a few days. That evening there was a grand ball and supper at the International Hotel at which two hundred of the ladies and gentlemen at the dejeuner attended.

The newspaper reports were peppered with the evidence of the material culture: clothing, carriages, hotels, five-foot wedding cakes and other food, an up-and-coming photographer, the implied status of the location and the guest list that demonstrated the cream of the social elite. Apart from the obvious mention of the bishop of Derry officiating, however, it is not obvious today that the names of the guests given were of the highest social ranking, but they would have been easily known within the readership of the *Irish Times* and the other papers in the close-knit society of the time. Although the number of guests seems large, the upper-class society at that time would have been like an extended family and indeed, in most cases, they were. The guests were family members, from the Conollys and Pakenhams themselves to the Shaws, Rowleys, Bruens, Ponsonbys and Napiers; other family members included the Taylors, earls of Headfort, while others such as Lord Cloncarty and the earl of Bessborough were close friends. With so many guests, the implied expense of the wedding reception and the ball in the evening revealed that a considerable sum of money had been spent on entertaining them at two separate events. This wedding ceremony and the attendant displays are a type of investiture with symbolic rites transforming the persons concerned. This is social magic and the more spectacle involved the greater the difference between the viewer and the participant.[66] These guests were not just rich and beautiful, they were the power brokers and they fashioned the social and cultural norms that constituted nineteenth-century society.

This was not the only celebration of the wedding on that day. Two newspapers reported another event at six o'clock that evening. This was held at the 'beautiful baronial establishment of Parsonstown House, immediately adjoining the walls of the highly ornamented demesne of Castletown, by desire of the illustrious owner of Castletown House'.[67] Conolly had instructed his popular agent Robert Cooper, who faithfully carried out the programme. The house was decorated and the tables were 'profusely furnished with every imaginable description of good things [and] were ornamented with the choicest plants and flowers from Mr Conolly's garden, and everything which could contribute to the enjoyment and happiness of the guests'.[68]

Today, this overtly complimentary language seems obsequious, but at the time this was the accepted approach. Reporters did not stop at complimenting the host, they also had to praise the guests chosen by the host and it is in this vein the following was written:

> A finer well-dressed, more temperate, or apparently, more well to do, class of warm-hearted tenantry we have very scarcely seen collected together as those, which it was our proud privilege to see assembled together yesterday evening.[69]

This effusive description of the guests was directed as a compliment towards Conolly, but one can perhaps hope that the observation was true. That Conolly would put on such an event speaks volumes with regard to the deference that he demonstrated to his tenants and employees.

This was not the end to the wedding celebrations. Two weeks after the wedding, the couple travelled to Donegal where in Ballyshannon the streets were hung with banners and flags and hundreds turned out. The town commissioners delivered an address to the bride and groom and this was 'replied to in feeling terms by Mr Conolly'.[70] This journey was not just for personal reasons. Conolly may have wanted to reinforce his ties with his tenants, but his political constituents had to be considered as well. He needed to perform his role as their MP, sharing with them a momentous event in his life.

On their honeymoon in Paris late in September, Conolly renewed his acquaintance with Napoleon III and such was the connection between the two men that Napoleon III gave them a gift of a pair of Meissen Jardinières that are still at Castletown today.

The recognition that Conolly's marriage was a significant event in the lives of those closely connected to the Conolly and Shaw families and other dependents was seen in another wedding-related event. In November, eleven weeks after their marriage, Thomas and Sarah Eliza came home to Celbridge. The couple had not been to Castletown since their wedding in September and their return was treated almost as part of the wedding celebration itself. Like Ballyshannon, the townspeople of Celbridge turned out to welcome them. The event was described by the correspondent of the *Irish Times*, who revealed it to have been a combination of reciprocal social contact between the Conollys and the local people, where there was another chance for Thomas to demonstrate his ties to the community.[71]

Between the train station and Castletown there were three triumphal arches and the town was festooned with flowers, banners and flags. On the first arch was inscribed *Cead mille failthe* (sic) and there they were met by a large concourse of people consisting of the inhabitants of the town, the tenants of the estate and the workmen of the two factories belonging to the Shaws, who had declared the day a holiday for the purpose of doing honour to the couple. At the second arch, which said 'Welcome', they were met by the band of the town, which played appropriate airs. The houses of the town were also decorated with green boughs and flags. Here, in the centre of town, a committee of nearly fifty persons received the procession where an address was read. On the last arch, at the gates of Castletown, were the words 'Safe, safe at home'. The assembly then proceeded up to Castletown House where Conolly addressed them in affectionate terms. That evening there was a large bonfire at the gate that was kept burning most of the night. The Conollys, who walked as far as the centre of the town and back again, 'amidst the hearty congratulations of the spectators', then witnessed a display of fireworks. Dancing then began around the bonfire and continued for several hours. One can speculate that if the family had not been held in such high regard it is unlikely the town would have gone into such lavish greetings. It must be acknowledged that the rent book of Castletown Demesne indicates that the entire town was paying rent to Conolly. Nevertheless, with fifty people on the committee, this would signify the general view was positive.

The symbolic power that was generated by the wedding and the three subsequent events in the newspaper reports served to reinforce Conolly's position in society. The status of the guest list showed the network of power that Conolly, and to a lesser extent that of Sarah's family, served to enhance the couple's own status. The second wedding celebration at Parsonstown, the event in Ballyshannon and, finally, the Celbridge homecoming would have contributed to the connection that the tenants and employees felt towards maintaining the lifeworld that Conolly had created and, along with others of his elite group, sought to control the cultural hegemony of Ireland. The expense of the wedding, the travel across to Donegal just to say 'hello', then more travel to Paris demonstrated more about leisure time and disposable wealth. Mobility itself is one of the significant markers for power and wealth.

Although socializing mostly took place in the private sphere, as the nineteenth century progressed dining and dancing outside the home were becoming acceptable in upper-class hotels. This is evident in the wedding reception at the International Hotel, but it was still important for women not to become too visible. Women were mentioned in the newspaper on only two occasions: their marriage and their death and, in this context, the marriage of Miss Sarah Eliza Shaw was the first time in her adult life that she was allowed to become visible. Men, on the other hand, were always highly visible.

2.8 Sarah Eliza Conolly (Rathdonnell Papers)

An early undated photograph of Sarah Eliza in the Rathdonnell family album is labelled 'Mrs Conolly' (fig. 2.8), while another from the early 1870s shows three of their four children: Thomas (1870–1900), Catherine (1871–1947) and William (1872–95) (fig. 2.9). No photograph of Edward Michael (1874–1956) was found.[72]

Nothing is known of Thomas and Sarah Eliza's life together until, according to Conolly's diary of 1870–1, the couple embarked on a grand tour of Italy along with their first surviving son, his nanny, a

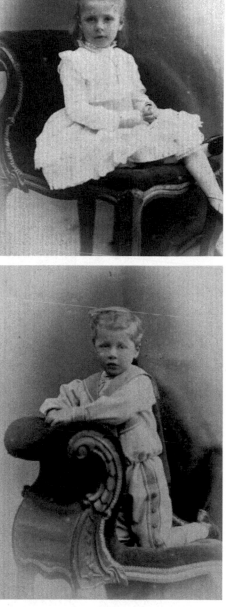

2.9 *From top left*, Thomas Jr (1870–1900), Catherine (1871–1947) and William Conolly (1872–95) (Rathdonnell Papers)

lady's maid and a valet. Conolly recorded an array of sights, as they traveled through France, Germany and Switzerland on their way to Italy. He wrote a commentary on his impressions of the ravages of the disastrous war with Prussia embarked upon by his friend Napoleon III, and from which France was only recovering. They savoured the cultural delights of Italy, and they stayed in Rome for several months. As they began their progress back to Ireland, they visited Florence, which included a tour of the Pitti Palace, a significant destination, thought to be the inspiration for the Red Silk Room at Castletown decorated by Conolly sometime after this tour.[73]

In the later years of his life, despite his buoyant personality and lifestyle, conditions had begun to change. Conolly's political career began to falter, he was re-elected with only a slim margin in the 1874 election and, because his health was beginning to be of some concern, had he lived he would probably not have stood at the next election. The *Leinster Express* confirmed his poor state of health when it reported that he had 'contemplated resigning his seat through ill health' and that he had been 'absent from parliamentary duties for some time'.[74] It is possible that his poor health was very serious because a note in his diary of taking mercury indicates that he had contracted venereal disease, which was not curable at the time.

The final general election of Conolly's career occurred following an unexpected dissolution of parliament by Gladstone. As a Liberal, he hoped to secure more seats by catching the opposition by surprise. In an open election letter to his Donegal constituents in January 1874,[75] Conolly mentioned the unexpected nature of Gladstone's decision but, despite this, he hoped for a re-election. This letter revealed his unionist allegiance when he stated that 'Home Rule is one full of delusion for our countrymen'. He noted that 'while it evokes all the noblest emotions of patriotism' it would create a 'servile dependent nation' without resources of its own: 'To this I would never consent'. This is a definitive answer regarding his position on Home Rule offered in the *Leinster Express* on his return from America.

During the early 1870s, newspaper articles show that he continued to have an interest in agricultural matters and was involved in hunting up until the year before his death. Newspapers listed the meets that occurred at Castletown during this period that included many aristocratic friends and other members of the Kildare Hunt among

2.10 Thomas Conolly, 1875 (Wikipedia)

them the marchioness of Drogheda, the earl of Clonmell, Lord Henry
FitzGerald, Alderman James Lambert, former conservative mayor of
Dublin and many more.[76] His continuing interest in hunting activities
was reflected in the alterations he made to the first floor of the east
wing of Castletown in 1871 as a clubroom. This room is evocative of
the hearty lifestyle that men and indeed women of the hunting set
enjoyed until well into the twentieth century, as later pictures of the
Conolly Carew family attest. As with the garden house, he employed
the leading architects of the day, Sir Thomas Newenham-Deane and
his partner Benjamin Woodward. The carved gargoyle-like rafters are
very reminiscent of Kilkenny Castle's picture gallery and St Canice's

Cathedral also in Kilkenny. By choosing these men he displayed his taste and sophistication.

There were, however, other signs that all was not well. Photographs (e.g., fig. 2.10) do not show a man in the full vigour of his health for someone aged 53. In February 1876, a sale of four hunters was advertised by Mr Sewell, a Dublin auctioneer who gave the reason 'as Mr Conolly is no longer able to hunt'.[77] In addition, on the eve of the Spring Show on 17 April of that year, there had been a large sale of stock from Castletown. This consisted of 'the most fashionable blood ... 14 cows and heifers and five bulls'.[78] To dispose of an entire herd and bulls would indicate that Conolly was moving out of dairying, which may have been precipitated by his declining health.

As mentioned already, there are hints in the diaries that Conolly had at some stage probably contracted venereal disease. This is the only reason he would have been taking mercury, as he noted in November 1853. In the weeks leading up to this reference he complained of feeling unwell, which could be the typical early flu-like symptoms and joint pains. Later on, he complained of throat pain, possibly the occurrence of inflamed lymph glands and weakness also due to the condition. His pre-marital promiscuity would have predicted such an eventuality and it would have been hard to avoid given his habit of seeking out sex-workers whenever the opportunity presented itself. His death certificate records 'Disease of the Supra-Renal Capsule' as the cause of death. This disease, now known as Addison's Disease, was brought about by the taking of mercury.[79]

Having venereal disease could have had implications for the health of both his wife and his children. Sarah Eliza lived until she was in her 70s, however, and apparently died of renal cancer. Although their second son William died of an illness in the mid-1890s, that appears very like leukaemia. With three out of her four children apparently healthy and well it is probable she had not contracted venereal disease. If Conolly had entered a latent or the tertiary stage of syphilis before his marriage, he would not have been infectious and neither Sarah Eliza nor her children would have been affected, otherwise she could not have avoided it.

Thomas Conolly died aged 53 on 10 August 1876. The *Irish Times* mourned him as

> genial, kindly, generous to a fault, patriotic in sentiment where
> the best interests of Ireland were concerned, and one of the very
> best of our resident landlords … his name was a household word
> for everything suggestive of benevolent consideration for the
> welfare of his numerous tenantry.[80]

The *Leinster Express* in the weeks following his death began
their obituary 'scarcely a living man who has in his own person
exemplified such a combination of pluck, enterprise, dash, adventure
and romance as was realized in the short career of the most esteemed
Irish gentleman' and concluded with 'His tenantry adored him.
Ireland was fond of him. We know of no other man of the time who
so completely and so artlessly gathered into his own individuality so
many of the characteristics which go to make up the ideal specimen
of the type of high-bred Celtic manhood'.[81] Several decades later,
in his son Thomas's obituary, a New Zealand paper recalled him as
'almost the last of the old school of Irish gentlemen – gay, gracious,
kindly, brave and chivalrous'.[82] His friend Lady St Helier summed
him up thus:

> dear old Tom Conolly … his hospitality was unbounded, and
> his house was always full. There were horses to ride, there
> were cars to be driven, there was an excellent cook and plenty
> of champagne … he was the kindest, the brightest, the most
> delightful of people, perfect as a host, a kind and staunch friend
> and universally beloved; and his memory is still green in the
> recollection of those with whom he came in contact.[83]

Like the Speaker, Conolly was originally buried in the family chapel
at Tea Lane cemetery, Celbridge. Only later were his remains moved
to the new family plot in the churchyard of Christ Church, Celbridge,
where a striking Celtic cross marks his grave (fig. 2.11).

The Conolly fortunes had already been in decline when Thomas
succeeded his father in 1849, the legacy of the family history, and
Edward Michael's will shows that he left Thomas only £10,000, a sum
his father indicated would barely be enough to sustain the estate.[84]
Details of any investments or financial matters about Castletown
during Conolly's lifetime are limited to slight evidence of three
household account books.[85] These books are only a small hint of the

bigger financial picture, seen through the landholdings in Donegal,
and they fail to provide any detailed clues as to how Thomas Conolly
was able to live as well as he did. Given the financial history of the
estate and Conolly's profligate lifestyle, it is likely that there were
considerable debts to be paid at his death. The final probate, proved
in 1877, left £25,000 to Sarah Eliza, but with no hint of the debts that
remained.[86] In recent years, a full copy of the will has been donated

> ## ROLLS COURT—Tuesday.
> (Before the Master of the Rolls),
>
> The Scottish Provident Institution v. Sarah Conolly, the Right Hon. Henry Bruen and others.
>
> The suit is to administer the real and personal estates of the late Thomas Conolly of Castletown, in the County of Dublin, who had large estates in that county, and also in the Counties of Kildare, Donegal and other counties, and who also owned a large quantity of family jewellery, furniture, statuary and plate, which he had devised as heirlooms, to be held by persons entitled to his settled estates.
>
> Mr. Bewley, Q.C., with whom was Mr. J. W. Richards (instructed by Messrs. Reeves & Son), on the part of the plaintiffs, who are mortgagees and creditors for over £100,000, applied for an order that an inventory should be made of the furniture, plate, diamonds and jewellery which are in the possession of Mrs. Conolly, the widow of the deceased, at Castletown, and that they should be sold and the proceeds invested for the benefit of the creditors. Counsel said it was manifest that there would be a large deficiency in the administration.

2.12 *Nationalist and Leinster Express*, 3 May 1890

to the Castletown Archive, but without financial figures. It sets out only the line of inheritance of his sons and daughter and instructions that, the 'heirlooms' aside, his real and personal property is to be sold to cover his debts. It mentions that, while Sarah Eliza's jewellery is to go to her, the 'family diamonds' must stay in the family. No further mention of these diamonds has occurred.[87]

Some fourteen years after Conolly's death, a newspaper article (fig. 2.12) and the law report concerning the financial situation of the family surfaced. In 1890, the year before her son's majority, Sarah Eliza appears to have been embroiled in a court case with the Scottish Provident Institution concerning complicated financial matters with a sum of £100,000 in mortgages mentioned. The Registry of Deeds (RD) also showed other mortgage sums of £1,361 and £3,500 involving the same institution and using the same land bank as collateral.[88]

The article disclosed that some but not all of the Castletown 'real and personal property' was entailed and that Sarah Eliza, in the years following Conolly's death, bought some of the personal property described as 'heirlooms' from the trustees. Three years later, in 1893, given the remarkable nature of the case it was subsequently written up in the *Law Reports* journal.[89] It appeared that in 1875, the year before Conolly's death, the Scottish Provident Institution, an insurance company, had provided a mortgage to Conolly of £98,000.[90] The collateral for the original mortgage was the entire Conolly land bank in Donegal, Dublin and Kildare. In addition, in the same year he took out two life-insurance policies, to the value of £20,000, which indicates he knew he was not well. While the 1890 newspaper report hints at the detail, the *Law Reports* explain it more clearly; Henry Bruen, Arthur Kavanagh and the solicitors William and Henry Cooper, having paid off some of the principal of the mortgage with the life insurance mentioned, re-mortgaged the lands for a further £17,000 in 1877, for a reason that is difficult to understand. This re-mortgage appears to be partly the basis for the court case in 1890. The court that year demanded an inventory of the contents of Castletown House with a view to selling some of the 'personal property'. This demand was due to the failure to pay off the interest on the mortgage either to the trustees or to the Scottish Provident Institution. While these two sources are deeply revealing about the ongoing financial circumstances of the Conolly household, they fail to reveal the underlying financial position.

In the years following Conolly's death, Sarah Eliza appears to have continued to live with her children at Castletown until after her eldest son's twenty-first birthday in 1891. The newspaper reports were fulsome in their description of a celebration that took place over several days at Castletown.[91] By 1895, however, financial pressure meant that she and her daughter Catherine had moved into other accommodation to facilitate the renting of Castletown. Moving to more modest accommodation would be the trend for the landowning elites as more and more were forced to sell their country houses. A combination of general financial difficulties and the changes in the late nineteenth century on the legislation regarding landholding led to reduced income as well as the sale of land.

2.13 Weekend house party at Castletown, *c*.1903 (Castletown Archive)

From *c*.1895 until the early twentieth century, Castletown was rented to several wealthy individuals, during which time it was once again used for lavish entertaining as it had been in the eighteenth century. The first was Sir Peter O'Brien, lord chief justice, and later, in 1899, Edward Kelly, son of an Irish-American banking family.[92] Later rentals, when it would see the hosting of the twentieth-century phenomenon of weekend parties, have not been publicly documented. A photograph (fig. 2.13) redolent with hints of just such an event in 1903 shows a group on the front steps of Castletown – some in hunting attire – before a meet of the Kildare Hunt. The group includes, in the centre of the picture, the hatless earl of Dudley, then the viceroy of Ireland.[93]

The following decade would prove challenging for Sarah Eliza. Two of her sons pre-deceased her: William, her second son, died in 1895,[94] and in 1900 her eldest son, Thomas, the object of so much idealized admiration, as the testimonials from his twenty-first-birthday celebrations showed, was killed in South Africa during the Boer War. The youngest son, Edward Michael, also fighting in South Africa at the time, survived. By the beginning of the new millennium, the 1901 census showed Sarah Eliza and her daughter Catherine living in St Austin's Abbey, Tullow, Co. Carlow, but eventually, around the time of the marriage of Catherine in 1904 to the Hon. Gerald Carew, the two women had moved to London.[95] Her son Edward Michael would later name Catherine and Gerald's son, William Carew, as his heir. Sarah Eliza Conolly died, aged 75, in 1921, one hundred years after the death of the memorable chatelaine of Castletown, Lady Louisa.[96]

Sometime in the 1920s, Edward Michael, Thomas Conolly's youngest son, returned to live on the Castletown estate and involved himself in some limited social events. He hunted with the Kildare Hunt, whose meets had continued to take place at Castletown, despite the house being rented out. Lord William Carew and his wife Lady Sylvia came to live at Castletown in 1938. As Edward Michael's health began to fail, Lord William and Lady Sylvia became his main carers. On his uncle's death in 1956, William Carew, like his great grandfather, added Conolly to his family name when he inherited. Without finances for dealing with the essential maintenance of an ageing eighteenth-century house, however, they did not find it an easy period. With the passing of time, Castletown was becoming a vast liability and, overwhelmed by the pressing difficulties, the family sold the house in 1965. This ended an unbroken 265-year association with the lands at Celbridge.

CONCLUSION

From the seventeenth century until the death of Thomas Conolly in the later nineteenth, the Conollys were typical of the aristocratic and landed families of the period. Although the Conollys were not originally Protestant, they switched fidelity sometime in the seventeenth century and became part of the Protestant ascendancy machine.

What was significant with the Conollys and across the power elites of the ascendancy class was the nature of their networks, the pivotal machine of authority driven through the presentation of a largely united front. The power of the family declined and the second Thomas Conolly played a small role in the overall social and political picture of Ireland. He was someone who would find changes to long-established patterns hard to embrace. He was not a man with any visible nationalist sentiments and had found it difficult to come to grips with the disestablishment of the Church of Ireland and the land reforms from 1870 onwards that would ultimately change the power structure of Ireland. Conolly's personal history straddles a transitional era; this chapter helps to understand the nature and extent of a certain power elite, the landed gentry, in Irish history with a particular focus on the mid-nineteenth century, and how not just then-current politics, but the inheritance of economic and social burdens from previous family generations crucially formed their world. The remainder of this study will contextualize Conolly's life as a connected individual in a wider network of influence through the landscapes of power in which he operated.

3. Thomas Conolly and the social networking of power

Conolly's networks form circular associations. The tightest circles move outwards in wider ripples to his weaker personal networks that are no less fundamental to his lifeworld. The locations closest to his two homes in Kildare and Donegal, his immediate source of resilience and support, were where he had the deepest personal contacts. These contacts become more sparse as he moved outward along the network. The diaries have shown the different scales of intensity of his networks radiating outwards to weaker personal contacts across his life. In London they seemed to be at their weakest but, as this chapter will show, this does not necessarily mean they were less active or less important.

The networking of the power elite was widespread and, beyond the domestic and governmental settings, could also be found in their mutual associations; educational, military and the Protestant church as well as gentlemen's clubs and many wider points of connection. The elites of society also had similar if not the same schooling and often married into each other's families. Social networks also developed beyond these categories within additional spatial settings where the aristocratic and upper-middle-class elites met and mingled: official government social events, sporting events and travel to fashionable locations. This included health resorts, where the social network spread out as one would expect to overlap with private life.[1] These more social forms of association are no less important in power-network terms.

Outside the official forms of tangible authority, a range of associations, clubs and sporting pastimes were a magnet to the elite and clubs of many types were the baseline from which the social network operated. Their overlapping, shared set of interconnections led to greater influence. Conolly's networks and 'interlinks' were large and both elite and multi-layered across the broad threads of education, clubs and the sport of hunting.

INITIAL ASSOCIATIONS: EDUCATION

To make the right connections within the network, an individual had to establish and maintain specifically personal contact with others in the same social sphere. This was accomplished initially by sending sons to the best 'prep' school followed by the best public school. The drive to develop the network for influential connection, to obtain a better position in the power structure, meant that joining the best regiment or the right club was the necessary next step to take advantage of the opportunities that connection to other influential people could provide.

Conolly attended Harrow, one of the two top English public schools, the other being Eton.[2] These educational associations were, in several respects, important foundations of the social network, facilitating the need for making the right connections in the network. One often hears of the phalanx of influence of 'old Etonians' or 'old Harrovians' or more generally 'old-boy networks' in the move up the social or corporate ladder by individuals in the twenty-first century, but this influence was multiplied considerably in the past, with a more powerful cohort of wealthy families. Conolly would have used the connections to the boys he met at school to give him a further entrée into English social life. After completing his time at Harrow, Conolly attended Christ Church, Oxford, for one year. Typical of the period, many students would not have completed a full degree. Going to university briefly was simply another box-ticking for elites, but his connection with Harrow and Oxford would have reinforced his connections in the elite gentlemen's clubs.

THE CHURCH AND THE MILITARY

After education, the two important public spheres of associational influence for the aristocratic network were the church and the military. The aristocratic and upper-middle-classes had close institutional links with the Church of England and the same was true of the Church of Ireland.[3] The Conolly family controlled the benefice of the parishes of Celbridge, Newcastle Lyons and Straffan. The living was given by Edward Michael Conolly to his uncle Revd Robert Pakenham who was still the incumbent when his son Thomas inherited in 1849.

Advancement in the church was significantly linked, both socially and financially, with the family members of the power elite, as it gave appropriate spiritual credibility and clergy were often at the forefront of formal social gatherings organized or attended by the elites.[4] The clergy in alliance with the landowners were significant local leaders and shared responsibilities for the community, particularly for the Protestant community, but of whatever religious persuasion for the very poor. The landlord and the clergyman were connected by a religious and social network that coordinated control over the local population regardless of religious denomination. It must be remembered too that the tithes, gathered for the benefit of the clergy, depended on every landowner in the country cooperating in paying this tax. The landowner, who had given the benefice to a chosen individual, also had a vested interest in the welfare of the particular clergy receiving the collected tax in the parish.[5]

For a great many elite young men who were of a robust nature, the military became a highly popular option, with their family's financial support. Members of the Protestant ascendancy dominated the Irish regiments of the British Army and their presence in the officer class replicated their managerial roles on the great estates. The certainty, as members of the aristocratic class, that the 'noble heroism' of battle was part of their inheritance, meant that they joined up as young men and often continued in the county militia.[6] The latter was a reserve force and typically where men gravitated, once they had finished with their regular army career.[7] Both of Conolly's brothers were in the army. Arthur Wellesley Conolly (1828–54) was a captain in the 30th Regiment of Foot and John Augustus Conolly (1829–78) was a Lieutenant Colonel in the Coldstream Guards. Both served in the Crimea, and John was awarded the newly instituted Victoria Cross (VC).[8] Their father Edward Michael was in the Royal Artillery and he served in the West Indies towards the end of the Napoleonic Wars, later becoming involved in the Donegal Militia. Significantly, these elite regiments remained in the United Kingdom during peacetime, thus avoiding the less-favoured Indian service. Many men after military service directed their efforts to the law, civil service or the church. Later in the nineteenth century, former military men with managerial skills might enter into business ventures, now becoming more acceptable for the landowning class. These church and military associations would have overlapped correspondingly with the networks operating through the other strands of the network, such as gentlemen's clubs, and the hunting calendar.

Conolly was never a member of the army or navy and there is no evidence that he was involved in the county militia either. His lack of military career is quite surprising considering his family tradition: his grandfather had been an admiral and had earned a knighthood in the service of his country, his father had been in the regular army and retired as a captain and later became a colonel in the Donegal Militia. Nearly all of the male members of Conolly's extended Pakenham family had been in either the army or the navy and, during the Napoleonic war in New Orleans, one had lost his life.[9] Conolly's adventures, revealed in the diaries of the 1850s and 1860s, and anecdotes by other elite authors, showed him to have been a physically active person and it is surprising he did not have a military career. In his 1864 diary, he lamented that, as the eldest son, he did not have the freedom to do as he wished and much of his life 'had been wasted in inaction or what strongly resembled it going round a profitless and uninteresting routine' and he envied 'the honourable paths of enterprise open to all younger sons and fortunate heirs of their own brains'.[10] However, he was being somewhat disingenuous, because there were plenty of examples of the eldest son having a military career, such as his own father and his Pakenham cousins. He must also have had sufficient physical presence himself because, on a visit to France in 1863, he participated in military manoeuvres with Napoleon III's army and later dined with high-ranking generals who appeared, as he reports in his diary, to readily accept his company.[11] Further evidence of his physicality and comfort in the military milieu is the ease with which he ingratiated himself with the military on his American adventure to the southern states. This experience suggests that he was comfortable in this male world and that his company was accepted by high-profile members of the military such as General Robert E. Lee (1807–70).

MARRIAGE

Generally speaking, the associations that marriage brought were fundamental in the social network. Marriage is itself a social institution and, in the context of the power elite, it served an important function. Conolly's marriage would have brought little in the way of increased networking except in the way that money provided a greater level of mobility and choices. Little is known about the Shaws' social connections except for the few clues in the guest list of the wedding. This included her grandfather, Revd Dr Pooley Shuldham Henry, the president of what would become Queen's University Belfast. Her father's sister Sarah had married the 4th Viscount Mountmorres, Hervey de Montmorency, who was dean of Cloyne, later dean of Achonry, and held the post of chaplain to the lord lieutenant of Ireland in 1853. The benefits of marriage worked both ways, however, and the position of Sarah's father and indeed her whole family would have been enhanced directly by her marriage into such a high-status family as the Conollys and, indirectly, the Longfords.[12]

DEEPER ASSOCIATIONS: CLUBS AS NETWORKED POWER BASES/HUBS

While the wider clerical and military networks were significant in themselves, it was clubs, of various types and status, that were of paramount importance in the networking of the power elite. It was important to join the right club to further one's social and political networks. The clubs of the greatest importance in Ireland, mainly located in Dublin, were the Kildare Street Club, the Royal Dublin Society and the Stephen's Green Club. There were various hunt clubs around the country, among them the Ward Union Stag Hounds and the Kildare Hunt. Some Freemason lodges were of high status and in Dublin the Merrion Lodge operating out of the headquarters in Molesworth Street was at the highest level of elite clubs. The rise of clubland and the development of the Dublin clubs with their affiliated interests had as their model the London-based St James Street/Pall Mall clubs.[13]

Elite gentlemen's clubs, separate from other less-exclusive clubs, were largely an urban phenomenon, and most tended to be part of a monopolistic group. Clubs were for dining, relaxing and meeting friends; one came into town to visit one's club. In their roles as sites of assembly, clubs allowed men, who were geographically dispersed across Ireland on their estates, to gather, socialize and conduct business. The clubs were the urban power hubs of the elite world, the power spaces that formed the foundation of a complex set of linkages. While socializing in their clubs, members shared their views on the establishment spaces in which they moved; they literally networked their power in place. A critical factor in the associational nature of clubs was their exclusivity.

ELITE GENTLEMEN'S CLUBS

From scattered references in his diaries, it was apparent that Thomas Conolly was a committed clubman. Conolly was a member of a number of elite and non-elite clubs, among them the Carlton Club in London, and the Kildare Street Club (KSC) and Royal Dublin Society (RDS) in Ireland. A conservative like his father, he was a member of the Carlton, noting regularly while in London that he 'dined at the club' that his father had co-founded. There are also references to Boodles, the prestigious London club.[14] At home in Ireland, he was known to also have been an habitué of the KSC. The centrality of his presence in the club scene is evidenced by the fact that

> between 1846 and 1876 Tom Conolly visited the club [KSC] once or twice a week for the express purpose of reinforcing guests under his huge rambling universally hospitable roof with some of its members who generally included Sir William Gregory.[15]

This wide-ranging hospitality was one of Conolly's defining characteristics. He was incredibly well connected and socialized with fellow KSC members outside the Kildare Street premises. He knew men both in the other Irish gentlemen's clubs, the hunt clubs and in the clubs he frequented in London. Eighty-eight men, around 12 per cent, from the KSC were also listed as members of the Carlton, showing the deep connective relationships between the twin nodes of Dublin and London. The high-status cultural activity enjoyed by members in wider society, enhanced by the greater friendship of strong club ties, provided the opportunity for families to engage with one another in other networked forms; facilitating, for example, possible marriage alliances.[16] Associations between individuals were

closely linked to those sponsoring them and helped further the
associations developed within the club setting by spreading outward
to other social settings. Conolly's diaries showed that many of his
social activities involved members of the KSC. In 1853 and 1857, he
recorded his attendance at Sir Gerald Aylmer's wedding and, while
in London, dinners, parties and balls with the Hamilton brothers,
Johnny and James, Lord Carew, Henry T. Clements and the earl of
Bective, all KSC members. Other men also fall into this crossover
of relationships: Sir Edward Kennedy, a KH hunt master, his cousin
William Ponsonby Baker and John Palliser, fellow blockade-running
planner, both friends and KSC members.

In Dublin's south side, the areas in the vicinity of Kildare Street were
the most fashionable, an extremely high-profile position both socially
and geographically, reflected in the location of Leinster House, the
town house of the duke of Leinster. The original KSC was located
in a building close to Leinster House. That cachet of association
extended to Molesworth Street, Merrion Square, FitzWilliam Street
and St Stephen's Green. With the elite development of St Stephen's
Green well established by the mid-nineteenth century, the University
Club was established in 1849 and soon after the Stephen's Green
Club would open only a few doors away. In 1860 the KSC erected a
prestigious building at the corner of Nassau Street and Kildare Street
(fig. 3.1).[17]

These building clusters were an outward representation of the
power elites, a demonstration of wealth and power, their very
geographical presence speaking clearly about the power of their
memberships. The most prestigious members built up an abundance
of visible honour and cultural capital by assuming the roles of officers
of the various clubs. The duke of Leinster was the grand master of the
Freemasons for sixty-one years, nearly his entire adult life. The earl
of Mayo became the president of the RDS. The third marquess of
Drogheda was on the committee of the KSC, as was Colonel Charles
Colthurst Vesey, a member of the notable Colthurst family of Cork.[18]

Essentially, it was those who were social leaders that would be
welcomed by the club; successful men from the highest levels of their
profession from public life. An example of this ethos was Arthur
Wellesley, first duke of Wellington, who, as prime minister, war hero
and member of parliament, was both honourable and a celebrity.

3.1 Kildare Street Club (after 1860) (Kildare Street and University Club Archive)

He was a member of the KSC and the Whig Club and belonged to a range of other London clubs. Club members, with status and material attributes including a 'public-spirited involvement in the issues of the day and willingness to accept responsibility' would be highly valued. This all diffused 'into an effortless supremacy' … a gentleman.[19] This profile fitted Conolly like a glove. At the elite level of society, in addition to those mentioned, many would be in positions of authority: MPs, county lieutenants, high sheriffs, magistrates, grand-jury members, poor-law guardians, usually the chairman or secretary, and, later in the century, presidents of the county agricultural fairs.

Memberships and high office among the elite ranged across several clubs. Some individuals belonged to up to eight clubs or societies, of various types, in both Ireland and England. The intensity of association was a clear message of networked power. The individual most highly networked through the clubs was Henry Moore, earl of Drogheda (1825–92), who was a member of four Irish clubs: the Freemasons, the KSC, the RDS, the Royal Irish club; and three London clubs: Carlton, Travellers and White's, as well as being a member of the Kildare Hunt and he was known as the 'prince of sport'.[20] In addition, from 1850 he managed Punchestown, the popular racecourse in Kildare, and was also affectionately known as 'the Prince of Punchestown', a valuable epithet given the 'adhesive' significance of horse racing and hunting as a social bond.[21] More significantly, during the period under study, there was a strong governance component, given the majority of the county lieutenants, deputy lieutenants, high sheriffs, justices of the peace and magistrates in counties all across Ireland were members of these clubs. This deepened a sense of a visible and important spatial concentration of that power. Looking at the KSC for 1850–70, of the 685 members, 220 had a specific education indicator and, of this cohort, 63 per cent attended university, 36 per cent went to Eton and 20 per cent attended Harrow. The remainder went to a variety of other public schools. In the overall total, university attendance was 20 per cent.

The majority of the KSC members were also members of other clubs: 58 per cent of the 682 members were identified as belonging to two or more clubs, some as many as six or seven. These prestigious London clubs ranged from the Athenaeum, Carlton, Boodles and White's to Travellers and the United Services Club. The high-profile clubs in Dublin were a mixture of respectable middle-class and high-status elite. What is important is that, in social networking terms, Conolly and his colleagues were socially networked deeply in Ireland, but also were linked into very influential networks in London and, by extension, these connections opened up an even wider geography of international connectivity, both within the British Isles and beyond, as witnessed in Conolly's diarized documentation of people he met and visited in Europe and America.

The depth of the social network was not just personal and social but also governmental and institutional. Indicating the reach of influence of KSC members, 85 per cent were identified as holding appointments and roles from MP to county lieutenant, high sheriff, justice of the

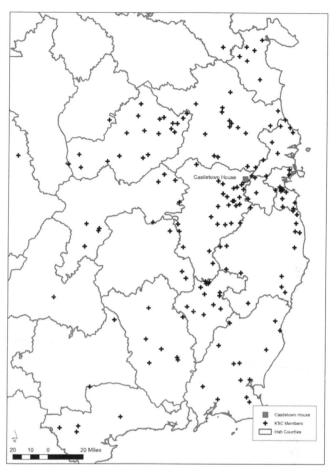

3.2 Kildare Street Club members in Leinster

peace, and magistrate. Others, as well as the appointments mentioned, were grand-jury members, poor-law guardians, privy councillors, or barristers and judges. Additionally, they held the positions of lord of the treasury and comptroller of the royal household and were the representative peers of Ireland. They were also trustees of Maynooth College, and directors of railway companies and banks. Most notably, however, if an individual was a member of a religious order, apart from his parish appointments, he was not involved in a civic role. In addition to the civic appointments; 28 per cent of KSC members held hereditary titles and this on its own contributed a high degree of status, but more significantly 68 per cent of those with titles held land over one thousand acres. That these lands were not necessarily all in one location showed the piecemeal spatial spread of landowning. The pervasive presence in the landscape of the high-status power elites of the KSC membership with their unified connectivity was one that had a significant impact on the control of everyday cultural practices in Ireland. In relational geography terms, it was the explicitly concentrated and connective nature of the club that produced such a hegemonic spatial web and, through both landholding and positions of authority, it cemented that network across the country.

Clearly, members of the KSC were landowners and the vast majority of them were owners of substantial property, a significant prerequisite for membership. Although the majority of KSC members lived in Leinster, the members were spread spatially across the country thus distributing their influence and networking nationwide.[22] The accompanying map (fig. 3.2) shows those KSC members living in Leinster. The more land one had the better for social and economic reasons, and this demonstrated the landowner's control over the local area. Depending on the individual, this usually meant that, as one of the power elite, he also held significant civic appointments. The parklands of the power elite varied in size and the income accruing depended on their location and the fertility of the soil. For example, the largest landowner in Ireland in 1872 was Peter Howe Browne of Westport, Co. Mayo, the marquis of Sligo. Because of the poor agricultural quality of the soil, however, his income on the 114,881 acres in Mayo was modest at £16,157 per annum. In comparison, the income of Henry Bruen, Thomas Conolly's brother-in law, with only 23,000 acres, was £17,481 per annum, with his lands in more fertile locations, mainly Carlow.[23]

By comparing the map of KSC members' homes in Leinster (fig. 3.2) with the houses and parklands in Leinster (fig. 3.3), it can be seen that the ownership and therefore control of the landscape by the power elites, both members and non-members of the KSC, was considerable in Leinster alone.[24] As an example of landownership in Co. Kildare, the 1876 survey of landowners showed that 48 per cent of the population owned 99 per cent of the land. In a further breakdown of the 1,766 Co. Kildare landowners, eighty-two owned one thousand or more acres of the total of 412,490 acres valued in the county. Forty of the eighty-two landowners in Kildare were

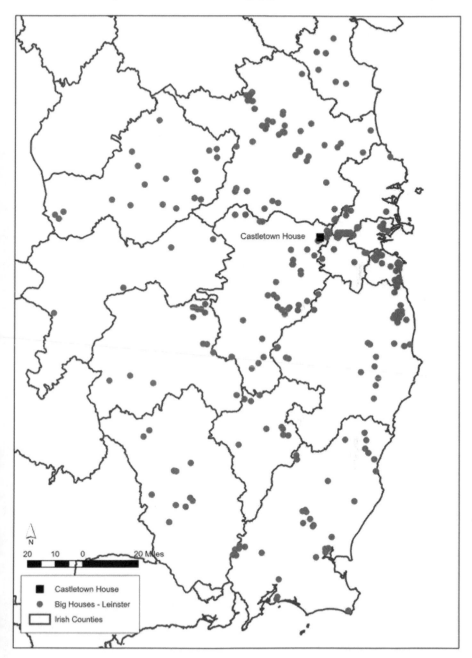

3.3 Distribution of parklands and demesnes in Leinster

members of the KSC, including Thomas Conolly, whose own holdings in Kildare totalled 2,605 acres, showing that his reach of connectivity was always reinforced by his membership of and relative prominence within the KSC.

OTHER CLUBS

During the nineteenth century, literary and scientific societies such as the Dublin Society had become popular. Archaeological and antiquarian societies were also established and flourished from the mid-nineteenth century, such as the Royal Society of Antiquaries of Ireland (RSAI) and the Kildare Archaeological Society. These societies were another important activity within the elite classes with the money and leisure time to travel to areas of interest. Many members of these societies were landowners who, conveniently, on their lands had a site of antiquity that could be excavated and where the society would then come on its annual outing.

These types of clubs, while elite, were not as exclusive, or at least as selective, regarding their membership. The Royal Dublin Society (RDS), the Freemasons and the University Club fell into this category, as did the RSAI. The less elite clubs therefore had a more eclectic mix of individuals, socially and culturally. Nevertheless, the clubs accepted as members only individuals described earlier as 'one of ours': aristocratic and gentry landowners, respectable, comfortably off individuals; professionals in medicine, law and banking as well as the clergy, all with a typical Victorian interest in improvement ranging from moral, scientific, scholarly and agricultural. These men, and women to some extent (within the antiquarian societies), were also interested in seeking out new methods of approaching old ideas. They were people who represented the nineteenth-century 'esteeming reason, order and light'.[25]

Outside the KSC, the two clubs that most attracted the (male) elite of society were the Freemasons and the RDS. The power elite were represented in the greatest numbers in the KSC. One significant club at this time was the hunt club. The hunt clubs, until the end of the nineteenth century, were a highly elite group made up mainly of aristocratic and landed gentry and ranged across the educational, military, club and other associational groups that linked members together. They drew on the associations generated in the elite urban clubs. In terms of social networking, they added an important informal and leisure-based layer. Hunt clubs were also important conduits, albeit more active and outdoors, shifting the geographies of power in wider circles, to the countryside and the parklands of the great country house.

THE KILDARE HUNT

The Kildare Hunt was a significant Leinster hunt club and its members were suitably high-profile including Squire Tom, an eighteenth-century hunt master, the la Touches, Lords Seaton and Milltown, Baron de Robeck, the earl of Clonmell and the quintessential sportsman, the earl of Drogheda.

Thomas Conolly was an enthusiastic member of the Kildare Hunt and his 1853 diary indicated that much of his time was taken up with this sport around Ireland and he reported hunting thirty days during the season to which he brought his own horses. This was often facilitated by the now-defunct local railway companies across the country on trains especially hired for the event. Conolly occasionally gave a brief commentary of his experience at a hunt meet:

> We arrive to a meet Rockfield close to Kells & I do not find my hunter owing to the regular irregularity of message communication in our country the rag way to do it is to send a Boy to bring back an answer. Well up comes L'Raux and (oh my little stars) offers me a mount. ... I find my horse dammed sticky – I hammer him & he goes as hard as nails. Clifton Lodge, find a fox who after running around the place & crossing the river twice makes his run for 40 minutes. I got away alone with the hounds & had some fun![26]

In 1847, he had taken part in the point-to-point at the Garrison Sweepstakes for the Hunt Cup, which was mainly for officers and Kildare Hunt members and was won by Mr Kirkpatrick. Conolly's light-hearted attitude to coming third in a field of four was shown in his comment regarding the quality of Mr Kirkpatrick's horse Clinker:

'we might as well have been mounted on donkeys'.[27] Conolly recorded that he owned twelve horses for his personal use; this high level of commitment to hunting would have involved a sizeable outlay for anyone, both financially and materially.[28] Indeed, the other diaries show that he seemed to have spent most of his leisure time in Leinster attending hunts, with the attendant point-to-point race meetings. Considering that this activity was parallel to his responsibilities as an MP in London, this represents a considerable amount of travel back and forth during the season.

In Conolly's diaries, among those whom he hunted with in Ireland were his brothers Robert and John and cousins Dick Taylor and the Pakenhams as well as his brother-in-law Henry Bruen, who were also KSC members. Other hunting KSC members were William Burton of Burton Hall and William Kennedy of Johnstown House, Enfield, the master of the Westmeath Hunt (WMH). What Conolly's diaries show is that, although he was mainly hunting in Kildare, he was also active around the counties of Meath, Westmeath and Donegal, which showed his expanded network. In addition, and significantly, hunt members also held high-profile civic authority positions: Sir Montague Chapman, master of the WMH, was the high sheriff for Westmeath: James Dease, a member of WMH, was the deputy lieutenant for Cavan. Conolly himself was a master of hounds of the Kildares in 1846 and his brother-in-law Henry Bruen MP, deputy lieutenant, high sheriff and justice of the peace for Carlow, was involved in all three clubs. Other individuals also KSC members who hunted with the Kildares were the deputy lieutenant of Kildare, Sir George Aylmer, and John G. Adair who, while also being deputy lieutenant for Kildare, spread his influence widely being at the same time a magistrate for Kildare, Laois and Tipperary.

These political connections serve to underline the fact that the hunt clubs were essentially Protestant in their ethos and represented in the most obvious public performance the central control of the countryside. The Bishopscourt Hunt based in north Kildare was largely under the leadership of the Ponsonbys (earls of Bessborough). Described as one of the foremost Whig families, in the eighteenth and early nineteenth century they 'used hunting as the cement for their support base'.[29] Bishopscourt, 10km from Castletown, had strong family ties with the Ponsonbys (Conolly's mother was a Ponsonby)

3.4 The Kildare Hunt at Bishopscourt, by Michael Angelo Hayes (1823–77)

and the social connections between the two houses were reinforced by hunting.

Membership of a hunt club combined with the key elite gentlemen's clubs was de rigueur. Hunt clubs on a national scale demonstrated through their performance in the physical landscape more than any other activity a form of control of the environment. The landowner laid down strict rules on how the landscape had to be managed to create the right environment for hunting and to encourage the breeding of foxes. This control was linked to both employment and rewards for the local farmers, who were not directly employed, and, under the weight of the hunt club activity across the landscape, was deeply bound up in cooperation with the farming community. This was not without its difficulties.

Hunting was inextricably linked to the social network and, just as strongly, to family connections. By the nineteenth century, socializing extended to hunt balls, puppy shows, house parties, breakfasts, steeplechasing and point-to-point races and entertainments, some directed towards fundraising. Conolly's pleasure in the hunt balls and the young women he meets are evident in his comments in the many exclamation points that accompany them. Socially, Conolly was engaged with the entertainments central to the hunt season and was present at the numerous balls. As in the train journeys he enthusiastically included in his diary, the names of young ladies he met at the balls appear with up to five or six exclamation points for each, depending on his level of enthusiasm. Included in the 1853 diary are passing comments on the people he rode or stayed with at these and shooting events. 'Shot rather well and dined well and drank well ... and danced 'til 4 o'clock at the Kells Ball ... excellent. Miss Coddington, Miss Stephenson, Miss Taylors ... our girls, Miss Fox all pretty'.[30] He hunted Enfield on 26 March and wrote 'Willy loses his temper & two foxes in the open' and that he needs to lose weight: 'I cannot eat owing to the weight requiring all my care to reduce [to] 12 stone being an everyday care'.[31]

The fact that hunting was full of risk and adventure is evident from the entry in the *History of the Kildare Hunt*, which mentioned Conolly: 'Ran from Levittstown to the Barrow and back to Covert again, across the Barrow and killed at Archdeacon Trench's. Tom Conolly nearly drowned swimming the river'.[32] As the reading of his diaries indicates, adventure appealed to Conolly and hunting was an important facet in his life, even managing to include it on holiday in Italy in 1870. In 1872 the first floor of the east wing at Castletown was reinvented, creating a clubroom over the stables for the après-hunt diversions for the Kildare Hunt. The social scene associated with hunting was the most important aspect of the hunt and, unlike the other networking hubs, the hunting scene included women and young children with a mixture of friends and family. This was where the networking of the members' lives came together most visibly and would facilitate advantageous social and political connections if not potential marriages.

In 1870/1, during Conolly's three-month holiday in Italy, he hunted in the Palatine Hills with a club based near Rome. In this his final diary, he described the horses, the chase, the fox and finally the villa where the meet concluded with enthusiasm and admiration.[33] Although no other record of this remains, it seems he was appointed the master of the Rome Hounds in 1872 and given a portrait of Pope Pius IX as a memento.[34] This appointment suggests that the reach of his social network was linked to shared leisure interests that acted as a sort of cultural 'currency' well beyond the British Isles.

Hunting also impacted on the wider general population of non-elite groups and was deeply embedded in rural seasonal customs for the farming community, who acted as an audience in the hunting landscape. The highly visible sight of the hunt members in their scarlet jackets racing across the countryside would have reinforced a form of cultural power on everyday life. The display of material wealth by the elite hunt in terms of horses and clothing demonstrated to the non-elite group the differences in lifestyle. This reinforced the perceived power of the performance where the geography of the landscape acted as a very large stage set.[35]

By the late 1870s, due to the negative financial impact of the agricultural slump of the time, changes began to occur and the Protestant domination of landownership started to weaken.[36] Reflecting this situation, the hunt clubs began to rapidly decline.[37]

CONCLUSION

Thomas Conolly has been mapped as sitting comfortably, prominently even, in a number of the key geographic and associational spaces. That strong position was cemented by his membership of several of the physically imposing elite gentlemen's clubs that represented high social and cultural capital for their members.

By mapping Conolly onto these clubs, we can place him directly into those spaces and connections of power. The influential associations and posts held by the KSC members in the political arena and other establishment institutions showed that the influence of the individual club members moved beyond the local into the national arena. This supports the argument that while the homes of the elite may have been geographically dispersed, their social, leisure and associational activities were tightly networked both spatially and culturally, as the map demonstrates (fig. 3.2). Their shared experiences of common cultural privileges and their interlocking estates established the cultural and political dominance of the area and beyond.

Conclusion

This study set out to assemble through a detailed analysis of the scant biographical material about Thomas Conolly, including his diaries and other primary and secondary sources, a form of biography. This demonstrated and mapped representative social networks for the dominant class to which he belonged. As the central focus of this social spatial network, Conolly also exemplified, through his spatial mobilities and social rituals, the ways that elites connected with wider social and political arenas that, in turn, sustained hegemonic social orders. This study has also looked at the geographies of Conolly's activities and their reflection of the lifestyles of other ascendancy landowners in Irish society. This allows us to understand how the hegemonic power of the Protestant ascendancy class worked through the institutional governance in place and how this was challenged in the second half of the nineteenth century. The post-Famine period was something of a hiatus before the storm of the last twenty years of the nineteenth century and, as a result, this provides an opportunity to examine the everyday life of the elites.

The Conolly family were involved in what we might now characterize as 'public service' and that pivotal role was evidenced in the 'flow and interconnections' between different social groups and different individuals, over time and space.[1] From the seventeenth century the Conollys were typical of the aristocratic and landed families of the period. Although the Conollys were not originally Protestant, they switched allegiance and became part of the Protestant ascendancy machine. The elite landowners, based on their family history and networks of connections, controlled the social and political landscape, as their position in society demanded. Their roles of duty, responsibility and authority were beginning to change radically with the rise in the later nineteenth century of the middle class who demanded a greater role in the running of the country. These demands, however, did not entirely sweep away the highly structured nature of society at this time.

It must be accepted that this study has limitations, especially in regard to the limited documentation of Thomas Conolly's life. If the record of his life had remained intact it would have been much easier to describe both in print and in imagery. Research for a biography is highly dependent on primary sources. Despite the scarcity of these sources, one can begin to join up the connective nodes of the network and the thin material can be brought together to produce a picture of the man. What remains of Conolly's life are the networks in their abstract forms and this is what has been discussed in the study. With a trickle of papers coming to light, in the future more work could be undertaken to widen his biography. Arguably, another individual with a better documented life to demonstrate the social networking of power would have been preferable, but to create a history of Castletown in the nineteenth century there was no other option. Until this study, no historical narrative has been written of the social, cultural, economic or political aspect of Castletown after 1821 or before 1956.

Throughout this study, using Thomas Conolly as a marker, the social network that facilitated the power network has been described. Similarly, while his diaries show a strongly fluid, social network operating, both thick and thin, the shadows and threats can be glimpsed in his life: parliamentary debates, the gradual dilution of the clubs, the need to 'marry down' for money, the reckless American escapade and his own risqué behaviour. This is the value of creating biography, and with this semi-biography of Thomas Conolly and his lifeworld, he acts as a prism through which we can view the power elite in the mid-Victorian period. It is hoped that this study will contribute a greater insight into the story of the house in the nineteenth century.

Epilogue

CASTLETOWN HOUSE AFTER 1966

The eighteenth-century story of Castletown – designed by Alessandro Galilei for William Conolly – is well known and the nineteenth-century family history has now been outlined. What is less well known is the twentieth-century history of the house.[1]

After Thomas Conolly III's twenty-first-birthday celebrations, Castletown for the next thirty-six years was largely rented. Following the death of his mother Sarah Eliza in 1921, however, Edward Michael Conolly, Thomas Conolly's youngest son, returned to live on the estate in c.1926. In the late 1930s Lord William Conolly Carew, Edward's nephew and heir, together with and his wife Lady Sylvia Maitland, came to live at Castletown. All were active members of the community. Edward, who died in 1956 age 83, lived at the end of his life in the house cared for by the Conolly Carews.

Involved with the community of old ascendancy families, the hunting, horse and racing set with similar family histories, the Conolly Carews were well known and well liked. Their daughter Diana is perhaps the best known of their children for her involvement in the Irish Olympic Equestrian team in 1968. The family's involvement with hunting and show jumping is also well known and the family continues to be involved in such pursuits today.

As the years passed it became apparent that the upkeep of Castletown was becoming a financial burden and difficult decisions would have to be made. Desmond Guinness, as a neighbour and friend at nearby Leixlip Castle, was well aware of their financial difficulties and was informed that the house would soon be put on the market. Desmond and his first wife Mariga had re-established the Irish Georgian Society in 1958 in the face of so much destruction of Ireland's built heritage and they, among others, were most concerned about the fate of this great house.

The sale of the house and demesne consisting of six hundred acres occurred in 1965, but the sale of the contents would not take place until some months later in early 1966. The purchaser of the estate was ostensibly Julian de Lisle, accompanied to the auction by Major Willson, then master of the Kildare Hunt. At this sale, of the house and estate, Guinness was the under-bidder. Subsequently, rumours circulated that de Lisle 'wanted to live in the house' but this changed and new rumours indicated that 'his intention was to turn it into a hotel with complete modernisation of the interior'.[2]

In the period following the sale, de Lisle disappeared from the record and it seemed that the sale had fallen through. Before the sale of contents in early 1966, however, a planning application to Kildare County Council was published in the *Irish Times* which sought permission to erect cottages, stables and ancillary buildings at Castletown and the applicant was the same James Willson who had accompanied de Lisle to the auction.[3] Reports began to circulate that the estate was to become an equestrian centre and a year later a notice appeared in the *Irish Times* that 'detailed specifications [are] now being prepared for equestrian centre and polo ground'.[4]

At the time of the sale of contents, in April of 1966, Lord Carew had indicated that some items, such as the bookcases specifically associated with the house, would not be included in the sale. Fortunately for the future, prior to the auction of the house and lands, Guinness had bought a number of important items, including the magnificent Murano chandeliers in the Long Gallery, and other significant items of furniture and paintings. The remaining contents were examples of the family's material goods from the eighteenth century and were scattered into private collections. An example of this are Robert Healy's paintings of the Kildare Hunt completed in 1768, which have not come up for sale since that time.

Having apparently successfully completed the sale of the house to Major Willson, the Conolly Carew family moved elsewhere. Despite the rumours circulating about the use of the house, Willson did nothing to secure Castletown and during the following year while it was left unattended some vandalism occurred. Fortunately, this was relatively minor and consisted primarily of a portion of the lead being taken off the roof and a few broken windows, but people became very concerned that serious damage would take place. Desmond Guinness, the Irish Georgian Society and other like-minded individuals, began to consider how the house could be saved. This concern resulted in the formation by early 1967 of a private trust, Castletown House Co. Ltd, largely based on a loan from Guinness's trust fund due to be paid out in the coming years. As a result, the house and 120 acres of land, that included the main Celbridge avenue, were purchased from Willson 'at a cost of £92,500'.[5] In addition, the lands immediately surrounding the great 1740 Famine obelisk project known as *Conolly's Folly* were also part of the purchase. Having rescued Castletown, it would remain under Guinness's stewardship until 1982.

Once the house was in Guinness's ownership, only a few months later, in the summer of 1967, the furniture, paintings and furnishings purchased by him were returned to the house and Castletown was opened to the public. This opening was largely due to work of volunteers who carried out some conservation and acted as curators and caretakers. The house was officially opened by Erskine Childers, then minister for trade and commerce, in June 1968. The house had never been entirely closed to the public, as the Conolly Carews had opened the house on occasions in the 1960s, charging an admission of 2s. 6d. in aid of parish funds. By 1970 Castletown – the first eighteenth-century house in Leinster to be open to the public on a regular basis – had become 'one of Ireland's foremost visitor attractions'.[6]

In the following years the house would become the headquarters of the Irish Georgian Society, with Guinness as president, and for the purposes of running the house the Castletown Trust was set up. The society would remain there for many years, finally moving out in 1983. 'During the tenure of the IGS, restoration work was carried out, with teams of willing volunteers'.[7] The IGS directed the staging of musicals, theatricals, festivals and balls to reawaken the house and to raise money. The house was also re-furnished in stages with appropriate furniture and paintings through donations or long-term loans, a situation that remains in place today. In the late 1970s the Castletown Foundation took over ownership and administration of the house, replacing the earlier Castletown Trust. The foundation, established as an educational trust, with an emphasis on the fine arts, continued the programme of restoration. The foundation carried out 'a role that was very dear to the heart of its future chairman Professor Kevin B. Nowlan' and that saw a series of educational events take place throughout the 1980s.[8] This included master art classes, a course in interior decoration and seminars on formal conservation practices. These were overseen by Prof. Nowlan, David Mlinaric, decorator and advisor to the English National Trust, the Knight of Glin, Richard Wood, John O'Connell, John Costello and John Cornforth.

Although it appeared on the surface that everything was going well, there were growing uncertainties about the land around the house, mainly the 13-acre field in front of the house which was still owned by Willson, but also the lands that he owned to the south-west of the house. These fears were brought to the fore when planning permission was obtained, despite protests at the time, for what is now the Castletown housing estate whose access is the main gate of Castletown's avenue. This and the subsequent estate of Crodaun Forest Park encroach on the parkland and the vista as it was envisioned in the early eighteenth century, and which is important to the enrichment of the setting of the house.

> The legacy of those planning permissions for housing develop-
> ment is still much in evidence today with the constant challenge
> of, on the one hand, doing what is necessary to secure the future
> of the house and its parkland, and, on the other, ensuring that
> the needs of the residents of the nearby estate are acknowledged.[9]

In the 1980s Willson sold the lands at the back of the house, posing an even greater threat to the historic landscape. Although the new owner of these lands is sympathetic to the integrity of the house, the Castletown Foundation, 'with great reluctance ... made an arrangement ... in return for support for limited commercial development [that] *c.*120 acres were transferred to the Foundation ... immediately to the rear of the house beyond the ha-ha'.[10]

The situation with the land averted, the first serious crisis for the foundation came in 1982 when Guinness, the then chair of the foundation, found that for personal reasons he needed to raise a significant sum of money. This necessitated him having to sell much of the contents of Castletown House that he had purchased in 1966 and 1967. In June 1983 he resigned as chairman and committee member because, as he would become a beneficiary of the foundation, this created a conflict of interest. As outgoing first chair, Guinness appointed Nowlan as his successor, who continued as chairman of the foundation until his death in February 2013. In the lead-up to the sale, Christies valued the contents, which included items bought by Guinness before the original sale in 1965, such as the iconic cabinet, reputedly Lady Louisa's bureau. The sale presented the foundation with a major challenge – it was vital to the story and maintenance of the house that the contents remain in situ – but Guinness gave them first refusal, with an extended timeframe for funds to be raised that eased the situation.

The foundation launched a public appeal to raise a sum of £750,000 for the contents, and hopefully an endowment to allow the foundation to carry on its activities. Raising money at this time in Ireland with such a poor economic climate was a daunting task for the foundation, made up largely of academics. Fortunately, there were a number of significant donors in the early days, among them the Kress Foundation, matched by a sum from Lord Moyne. By 1984, assisted by a lottery, the fund had achieved nearly £200,000 but far short of what was required. Nevertheless, as time went on many items were secured with help from individuals, chapters of the IGS abroad and Bord Fáilte. Among the many paintings and furniture acquired were the Chippendale sofas and chairs, the Murano chandeliers in the Long Gallery and the Chatterton Smith copy by Reynolds of Lady Louisa. Retaining the original furniture and material goods provided an important link to the lifestyle of the eighteenth and, to some extent, the nineteenth century, of Castletown and the Conollys.

Despite enthusiasm and dedication, by the early 1990s the foundation began to experience the reality of keeping an eighteenth-century house in good order. The cost of maintenance was outstripping the foundation's ability to pay for the expensive repairs needed. The roof in particular was a major concern and its estimated cost was in the region of £3 million and, although 'a grant was given by the EEC, matched by the National Lottery for the restoration of the colonnades', much more was required.[11] As a private trust, the foundation was not able to directly apply to the EEC for funding, as this was only open to state agencies. As a state agency, the Office of Public Works were best placed to apply for a grant and the Castletown Foundation opened negotiations with this body to secure the future of the house. The official handover took place on 20 January 1994 when Nowlan presented the symbolic key to the then minister for arts and culture, Michael D. Higgins, later president of Ireland. Unique among heritage sites in Ireland under the ownership and management of the OPW, the foundation continues to play a significant role in the conservation of the house and the control and display of the contents.

Under the auspices of the OPW, the fabric of the building has been secured for the coming centuries. There has been a new roof installed, the colonnades have been restored and the wings have been remade into spaces suitable for the use of the visiting public. The interior spaces have undergone significant conservation and the contents have now been placed in a regime of conservation, ensuring they will also be maintained into the foreseeable future.

The only difficulty that remains are the lands that surround the house, which are outside the immediate control of the state and the foundation. They include the remaining parkland and the lands beyond. The setting for the house in the Liffey Valley landscape has been encroached upon by the ever-expanding conurbation of the Dublin suburbs consuming the small towns in the area. The woods within the demesne, the lands at the back of the house as well as the lands on the opposite side of the Liffey continue to be at risk of being developed and ongoing resistance is in place by the foundation, the OPW and other interested parties. It would 'be a travesty for Castletown, especially in the light of the conservation/restoration work in the landscape', which has been completed, if the surrounding 'borrowed' landscape, which is so significant for the setting of the house, should be lost.

Castletown continues to be a popular destination for visitors interested in heritage buildings, parks and a variety of staged events from musicals to markets. 'The Castletown Foundation, working closely with the OPW, continues its educational activities and uses its expertise and experience to work towards the ongoing conservation and sustainable use of Castletown, the house and its landscape'. The engagement of the public with this significant landscape of power speaks well of the openness of society today and perhaps holds echoes of the hospitality of Thomas Conolly II.

Notes

ABBREVIATIONS

ADC   Aide-de-camp
EEC   European Economic Community
IGS   Irish Georgian Society
KH   Kildare Hunt
KSC   Kildare Street Club
NAI   National Archive of Ireland
NLI   National Library of Ireland
OPW   Office of Public Works
RDS   Royal Dublin Society
RSAI   Royal Society of Antiquaries of Ireland
VC   Victoria Cross
WMH   Westmeath Hunt
WUH   Ward Union Hunt

1. THE CONOLLYS AND CASTLETOWN HOUSE

1   Patrick Walsh, *The making of the Irish Protestant ascendancy: the life of William Conolly, 1662–1729* (Woodbridge, 2010), p. 39.

2   Ibid., p. 22.

3   Jointure: a sole estate settled on a wife, following the death of her husband, during her lifetime: OED (1973). This in effect prevented Castletown being touched by William Conolly's heir William Jr until after the death of Katherine in 1752. In many instances, the heir benefited immediately, allowing the widow to remain in residence only at his/her discretion.

4   A.P.W. Malcomson, 'The fall of the house of Conolly' in Allan Blackstock and Eoin McGinnis (eds), *Politics and political culture in Britain and Ireland, 1780–1850* (Belfast, 2007), pp 107–56.

5   Walsh, *The life of William Conolly*.

6   Malcomson, 'The fall of the house of Conolly'.

7   A.M. Keller, 'The Long Gallery of Castletown House', *Bulletin of the Irish Georgian society*, 22 (1979); D.J. Griffin, 'Castletown, Co. Kildare: the contribution of James, first duke of Leinster' in Sean O'Reilly (ed.), *The Journal of the Irish Georgian Society*, 1 (1998).

8   Malcomson, 'The fall of the house of Conolly'.

9   Stephen Farrell, 'Edward Michael Pakenham Conolly' in D.R. Fisher (ed.), *The history of parliament: the House of Commons, 1820–1832* (Cambridge, 2009).

10 Admiral Hon. Sir Thomas Pakenham was born in 1757. He married Louisa Ann Staples daughter of Rt Hon. John Staples and Harriet Conolly, on 24 June 1783. He died on 2 February 1836. He was member of parliament (MP) for Longford between 1783 and 1790. He was also MP for Kells and Longford. He gained the rank of admiral of the red. He held the office of master-general of the ordnance [Ireland]. He was invested as a Knight Grand Cross, Order of the Bath (GCB).

11 Admiral Hon. Sir Thomas Pakenham was described in a letter to the *Irish Times* editor at the time of his grandson's death in 1876 as a 'cherry, warm-hearted rough old gentleman, [who] endeared himself

to the common people by entering into familiar conversation with them in their cottages and by the wayside ... he would hand an old woman over a stile ... just as heartily as a young countess to spring into her saddle': *Irish Times*, 22 Aug. 1876.

12 Farrell, 'Edward Michael Pakenham Conolly'.

13 NAI Thomas Conolly's will: 27 May 1799, T17412.

14 Lady Louisa to Lady Sarah, 1782. Castletown Archive. I am indebted to Nicola Kelly of Castletown Archive for pointing this letter out to me.

15 It appears that this house was in the ownership of Sir Thomas Pakenham's two granddaughters Harriet and Frances Conolly around the time of Thomas Conolly's death: *Landowners of Ireland 1876: return of owners of land of one acre and upwards in the several counties, counties of cities and counties of towns in Ireland* (Dublin, 1876; repr. Baltimore, MD, 1988), p. 83.

16 NLI Royal Licence 27 Aug. 1821.

17 His responsibilities extended to three parishes: Celbridge, Straffan and Newcastle Lyons. The modest rectory was located in Straffan, 8km from Celbridge.

18 Castletown Archive and NLI Conolly Papers MS 14,342.

19 A substantial house, Cliff was demolished in 1958/9. It was situated close to where the Ballyshannon Hydroelectric station on the River Erne is presently located.

20 *Belfast Newsletter*, 4 Jan. 1849.

2. THOMAS CONOLLY, 1823–76

1 Lena Boylan, 'The Conolly family, Dublin', *Irish Georgian Society Bulletin*, XI:4 (Oct.–Dec. 1968), p. 44.

2 Thom's Directory (1874) also listed Carrig Lodge, Killybegs, Co. Donegal, as a residence.

3 K.T. Hoppen, *Elections, politics and society in Ireland, 1832–85* (Oxford, 1984).

4 House of Commons' Debates, 26 Apr. 1869 (Irish Church Bill), cols 1613–14.

5 House of Commons' Debates, Irish Land Bill: Question 10 Mar. 1870 [cols 1621–1732].

6 'In the 17th century the foundations for *habeas corpus* were: no freeman shall be taken or imprisoned, or be disseized of his freehold, or liberties, or free customs, or be outlawed, or exiled, ... but by lawful judgment of his peers, or by the law of the land'. In other words, judgments passed by a court of law were necessary for imprisonment of individuals (Constitution Society available at www.constitution.org/eng/ habcorpa.htm; accessed 23 Apr.l 2015).

7 House of Commons' Debates, Peace Preservation (Ireland) Bill 1870, 17 Mar. 1870 (Habeas Corpus Act 1870), col. 112.

8 House of Commons' Debates, Peace Preservation (Ireland) Bill 1870, 17 Mar. 1870, col. 111.

9 Virginia Crossman, *Politics, law and order in nineteenth-century Ireland* (Dublin, 1996), p. 36.

10 Electoral County Boards (Ireland) Bill [Bill 8] 1876, cols 772–7.

11 J.C. Beckett, *The Anglo-Irish tradition* (London, 1976), p. 111.

12 R.V. Comerford, 'Ireland, 1850–1870: post-Famine and mid-Victorian' in W.E. Vaughan (ed.), *New History of Ireland: Ireland under the Union, 1801–1870*, v (New York, 1989).

13 *Leinster Express*, 19 Aug. 1876.

14 Conolly Diaries, 3 Mar. 1853.

15 Conolly Diaries, 24 May 1853: MS in the possession of Desmond Guinness: private collection.

16 M.J. St Helier, *Memories of forty years* (London, 1909).

17 Now the American Ambassador's residence in the Phoenix Park.

18 Joseph Robins, *Champagne and silver buckets* (Dublin, 2001).

19 Mark Bence-Jones, *Twilight of the ascendancy* (London, 1987), p. 44.

20 Thomas Conolly's mother and sisters: *Daily Express*, 4 Feb. 1851.

21 Ann Chambers, *At arm's length: aristocrats in the Republic of Ireland* (Dublin, 2004), p. 44.

22 Castletown Accounts, 1863–7: May 1864. Castletown Archives.

23 Maeve O'Riordan, 'Leisure with a purpose: women and the entertaining practices of the Irish landed elite, *c.*1860–1914' in Leeann Lane and William Murphy (eds), *Leisure and the Irish in the*

nineteenth century (Liverpool, 2016), pp 209–25 at pp 214–16, 225.

24 Conolly Diaries, 24 Mar. 1853.

25 Possibly born June 1822.

26 *The Giaour, a fragment of a Turkish tale by Byron.* Conolly Diaries, 26 Nov. 1853.

27 Conolly Diaries, 26 Nov. 1853.

28 Conolly Diaries, 29 July–21 Aug. 1863.

29 Boylan, 'The Conolly family', p. 45. The prize was apparently a copy of da Vinci's *Mona Lisa* by Luini: Sarah Conolly-Carew, *The children of Castletown* (Dublin, 2012), p. 66.

30 *Otago Witness* [New Zealand], 14 Nov. 1900.

31 Matthew Johnson, *Beyond the castle gate: medieval to Renaissance* (London, 2002), p. 12.

32 Uncatalogued papers: Castletown Archive.

33 Account Books, 1862–7: Castletown Archive.

34 Ibid. Only a small portion of this garden remains intact following the sale of the demesne in 1967, and the construction of a housing estate in the general area.

35 Maeve O'Regan, 'Nineteenth-century Renaissance Castletown's garden house and walled garden', *Journal of the County Kildare Archaeological Society*, 20:3 (2012–13), p. 277.

36 H.H. Gerth and C. Wright Mills (eds), *From Max Weber* (New York, 1958), p. 187.

37 Terence Dooley, *The decline of the big house in Ireland, 1860–1960* (Dublin, 2001), p. 44.

38 S.M. Pegley, 'Landscapes of power' (PhD, MU, 2017). This map and other maps were developed as mapped output from queries carried out on the database developed for the study.

39 N.D. Lankford (ed.), *An Irishman in Dixie: Thomas Connolly's diary of the fall of the Confederacy* (Columbia, SC, 1988).

40 Letter to Conolly from Emily Barton, 6 Nov. 1864 (IAA 98/79).

41 I.M. Spry, 'John Palliser' in *The Dictionary of Canadian Biography*, 11 (2003), www.biographi.ca (accessed 17 Jan. 2015).

42 Lankford, *An Irishman*, p. 10.

43 Conolly's Diary, 1864–5, 8 Dec. 1864 (IAA 98/79 and log book 1864–5 IAA A00073).

44 Log book 12 Dec. 1864 and Conolly's Diary, IAA.

45 Lankford, *An Irishman*, p. 104.

46 Ibid.

47 Sherman's March, www.history.com/topics/american-civil-war/shermans-march (accessed 24 June 2017).

48 C.E. Scott, 'Coping with inflation: Atlanta, 1860–1865', *Georgia Historical Quarterly*, 69:4 (winter 1985), pp 536–56.

49 T.N. Conrad, *The rebel scout: a thrilling history of scouting life in the southern army* (Washington, DC, 1904).

50 Lankford, *An Irishman*, p. 130.

51 Ibid., p. 124.

52 Ibid., p. 14.

53 Lankford, *An Irishman*, p. 127.

54 Letter 10 Nov. 1865, Conolly MSS, TCD.

55 *Irish Times*, June 1867.

56 Martina O'Donnell, 'The estate system of landholding in Co. Donegal' in Jim MacLaughlin and Sean Beattie (eds), *An historical, environmental and cultural atlas of County Donegal* (Cork, 2016), p. 246.

57 Ibid.

58 Walsh, *The life of William Conolly*.

59 A.P.W. Malcomson, *The pursuit of the heiress: aristocratic marriage in Ireland* (Belfast, 2006).

60 This amount represented a spending value of c.£1,204,874 in 2022: www.officialdata.org/uk/inflation/1 (accessed 5 Apr. 2022).

61 Boylan, 'The Conolly family'.

62 Law Reports (Ireland), 31 (1893), pp 329–37.

63 *Weekly Irish Times, Irish Times, Freeman's Journal, Leinster Express*.

64 *Irish Times*, 2 Sept. 1868.

65 A search of the NLI Lawrence Collection showed no record of these photographs.

66 Pierre Bourdieu, *Language and symbolic power*, trans. G. Raymond, M. Adamson and J.B. Thompson (4th ed., Cambridge, 1997), p. 121.

67 Parsonstown House, a house of the middling size torn down c.1980s/90s. The site was occupied first by Irish Meat Packers and later by Hewlett-Packard.

68 *Leinster Express*, 9 Sept. 1868.

69 *Irish Times*, 9 Sept. 1868.

70 *Leinster Express*, 28 Sept. 1868.

71 *Irish Times*, Nov. 1868.

72 Rathdonnell Papers, Lisnavagh House. Thomas born 1870, died 1900 in South Africa at the surrender of the Boer War; Catherine born 1871, died 1947, married Lord Gerald Carew, 5th Baron Carew in 1904; William born 1872, died 1895; Edward Michael born 1874, died 1956.

73 Conolly's Diary, 1870–1 (IAA 98/79, 1864–7); Penelope Jenkins, 'The Red Silk Room at Castletown' (MA, UCD, 2016). Also available at researchgate.net/ publication.

74 *Leinster Express*, 3 June 1876.

75 This letter was sent to me by the librarian of the law library at Blackhall Place. I have been unable to contact the librarian to provide a specific citation.

76 *Irish Times*, 19 Feb. 1875.

77 *Leinster Express*, 8 Feb. 1876.

78 *Freeman's Journal*, 8 Apr. 1876.

79 Mercury had terrible side effects, causing, among other things, kidney failure, severe mouth ulcers and loss of teeth. Penicillin was not introduced as a treatment until 1943.

80 *Irish Times*, 11 Aug. 1876.

81 *Leinster Express*, 19 Aug. 1876.

82 *Otago Witness* [New Zealand], 14 Nov. 1900.

83 St Helier, *Memories of forty years*, p. 59.

84 Last will and testament of Edward Michael Pakenham Conolly (1789–1849) (NLI T17411).

85 Account books relating to Castletown: 1828, 1830–9, 1860–9 (NLI Conolly Papers, MS 14,342).

86 This amount represents a spending power of c.£3,073,659 in 2022: www.officialdata. org/uk/inflation (accessed 5 Apr. 2022); NA Will Book 1877 entry 381.

87 Last will and testament of Thomas Conolly, 4 Nov. 1872, Castletown Archive. In conversation with the family, they have no knowledge of these diamonds.

88 Registry of Deeds, 1875, 14:107 and 108. Such are the numbers of memorials connected to Thomas Conolly in the RD that there is great scope for further work on Conolly's land transactions.

89 *Law Reports* (Ireland), 31, Master of Rolls (1893), pp 329–37.

90 This amount represents a spending power of c.£12,048,745 in 2022: www. officialdata.org/uk/inflation (accessed 5 Apr. 2022).

91 *Kildare Observer*, 6 Sept. 1891; *Leinster Express*, 6 Sept. 1891.

92 *Evening Herald*, 10 Oct. 1899.

93 This photograph is dated 1903. The caption on the back lists some individuals; from left: Henry Earl de Robeck, Mrs More O'Farrell, the Countess of Dudley, Dermot Earl of Mayo, Earl of Dudley, Viceroy of Ireland, Lord Ulster, Mrs Dalgaty of Ryevale House, Leixlip, Geraldine Countess of Mayo and Sir H. Bellingham. All but 'Ulster' is confirmed. Found by the author in Castletown House during a 'clean-out' c.2005.

94 William Conolly's death certificate did not indicate the underlying cause of his symptoms. The details on his death certificate – ulcerative endometriosis, anaemia, purpura and asthma – suggest either Rheumatic fever or some form of cancer, possibly leukaemia. General Register Office, England: registration district Kensington, sub-district of Brompton, county of London. Death certificate: William Conolly, 17 June 1895, vol. 01A, p. 112 (acquired 14 June 2017, application no. 8349152–1).

95 *Kildare Observer*, 7 May 1904.

96 The cause of Sarah Eliza's death was renal cancer: General Register Office, England, district Brentford, sub-district Chiswick, county of Middlesex. Death certificate: Sarah Eliza Shaw, 9 Oct. 1921, vol. 03A, p. 207 (acquired 18 Sept. 2017, application no. 581347–1).

3. THOMAS CONOLLY AND THE SOCIAL NETWORKING OF POWER

1 Ronan Foley, *Healing waters: therapeutic landscapes in historic and contemporary Ireland* (Farnham, 2010).

2 Other English public schools are Bedford, Charterhouse, Cheltenham, Marlborough, Rugby, Repton, Stonyhurst, Winchester and Westminster (R. Greaves, *A short history of the Ward Union Hounds* (Dublin, 1929), p. 174). Only Eton, Harrow and Rugby appear with regularity in the main database.

3 This would end with the Disestablishment of the Church of

Ireland in 1869. In future, incumbents would be determined by the Church of Ireland's own governing body, the Representative Church Body.

4   F.M.L. Thompson, *English landed society in the nineteenth century* (3rd ed., London, 1980).

5   Ibid., p. 5.

6   Chambers, *At arm's length*, p. 137.

7   Ibid., p. 112. Between 1854 and 1889 17.5 per cent of the officer class in the British army were 'members of the ascendancy'.

8   John Augustus Conolly was a son of Edward Michael Conolly MP and Catherine Jane Ponsonby. Born at Castletown House, Celbridge, he was educated at King Edward's School, Birmingham. He achieved the rank of lieutenant colonel. He married Charlotte Burnaby and had several children (thepeerage.com; accessed 8 Mar. 2022).

9   E. Pakenham, *Soldier, sailor: an intimate portrait of an Irish family* (London, 2007).

10   Conolly Diaries, 5 Dec. 1864.

11   Conolly Diaries, 19 July 1863.

12   Thompson, *Nineteenth-century society*, p. 19.

13   James Kelly and M.J. Powell (eds), *Clubs and societies in eighteenth-century Ireland* (Dublin, 2010). Also R.B. McDowell, *Land and learning: two Irish clubs* (Dublin, 1993).

14   Conolly Diaries, 1853/57/63. Originally known as *Almack's*, famous for dining and dancing, well known to readers of Jane Austen.

15   T.H.S. Escott, *Club makers and club members* (London, 1914), p. 332. This reference to 'roof' is one of abstract overarching hospitality not specific to any location. This man is Sir William Gregory, governor general of Ceylon, MP for Galway and Dublin.

16   D.E. Kendall, *Members only: elite clubs and the process of exclusion* (Plymouth, 2008), p. 116.

17   Sold in the 1970s, the interior was gutted and now houses the Alliance Française.

18   KSC Membership Lists, 1850–80: the Kildare and University Club, Dublin.

19   McDowell, *Land and learning*, p. 31.

20   Ibid., p. 54.

21   Richard Burke Earl of Mayo and W.B. Boulton (eds), *A history of the Kildare Hunt* (London, 1913), p. 345.

22   The History Department of NUI Galway have created a significant database 'The Landed Estates of Ireland' that covers Ulster, Munster and Connacht (available at www.landedestates.ie).

23   John Bateman, *The great landowners of Great Britain and Ireland: a list of all owners of three thousand acres and upwards* (London, 1883) (www.kessinger.net, 2009).

24   For a map of all parklands in Ireland, 1830 to 1900, see F.H.A. Aalen, K. Whelan and M. Stout (eds), *Atlas of the rural Irish landscape* (Cork, 1997), p. 202.

25   Elizabeth Bowen, *Bowen's Court* (London, 1942), p. 31.

26   Conolly Diaries, 13 Jan. 1853.

27   Mayo, *Kildare Hunt*, p. 181.

28   Conolly Diaries, 1863.

29   M.J. Powell, 'Hunting clubs and societies' in Kelly and Powell (eds), *Clubs and societies in eighteenth-century Ireland*, p. 407.

30   Conolly Diaries, 12 Jan. 1853. Miss Coddington was a member of the Coddington family of Oldbridge, Co. Meath, the site of the Battle of the Boyne, and the Misses Taylors are the daughters of the earl of Headfort.

31   Conolly Diaries, 26 Mar. 1853.

32   Mayo, *Kildare Hunt*, p. 195.

33   Conolly Diaries, 12 Dec. 1870.

34   Castletown 1893/4 inventory: transcription Dorothea Depner: annotated with sale results from 1966 sale (unpublished report, 2016). The auction catalogue (1966) noted that Conolly was given the painting 'Pope Pius IX' by D'Arti in 1872 when he was appointed Master of the Rome Hunt. There is no corroborating evidence of a visit to Italy in 1872 and this may have been an honorary title.

35   Toby Barnard, 'Integration or separation? Hospitality and display in Protestant Ireland, 1660–1800' in L. Brockliss and D. Eastwood (eds), *A union of multiple identities: the British Isles, c.1750–c.1800* (Manchester, 1997), pp 127–47.

36   Dooley, *The decline of the big house*.

37   C. Wright Mills, *Power elites* (7th ed., New York, 1956), p. 21.

CONCLUSION

1 Doreen Massey, 'A global sense of place', *Marxism Today* (1991), pp 24–9 at p. 25.

EPILOGUE

1 Jeanne Meldon Walsh, 'The story of a trust and its collection' (unpublished lecture, 2013). I am grateful to Jeanne who allowed me to quote from her lecture notes for this epilogue.
2 Ibid.
3 *Irish Times*, 8 Feb. 1966.
4 Meldon Walsh, 'The story of a trust'.

5 Robert O'Byrne, *The Irish Georgian Society: a celebration* (2008), p. 66.
6 Ibid.
7 Meldon Walsh, 'The story of a trust'.
8 Ibid.
9 Ibid.
10 Meldon Walsh, 'The story of a trust'. A 'ha-ha' is a half-walled ditch in a parkland that separates fields. Intended to allow viewers, usually from the vantage point of the house, to have an apparently unbroken flow of land, despite the fields being divided.
11 Ibid.